# As My World Still Turns

# AS MY WORLD STILL TURNS

## THE UNCENSORED MEMOIRS OF AMERICA'S SOAP OPERA QUEEN

Eileen Fulton
with Desmond Atholl and Michael Cherkinian

A BIRCH LANE PRESS BOOK
Published by Carol Publishing Group

A Birch Lane Press Book
Published by Carol Publishing Group
Birch Lane Press is a registered trademark of Carol Communications, Inc.
Editorial Offices: 600 Madison Avenue, New York, N.Y. 10022
Sales and Distribution Offices: 120 Enterprise Avenue, Secaucus, N.J. 07094
In Canada: Canadian Manda Group, One Atlantic Avenue, Suite 105,
Toronto, Ontario M6K 3E7
Queries regarding rights and permissions should be addressed to
Carol Publishing Group, 600 Madison Avenue, New York, N.Y. 10022

Carol Publishing Group books are available at special discounts for bulk
purchases, sales promotions, fund-raising, or educational purposes. Special
editions can be created to specifications. For details, contact Special Sales
Department, Carol Publishing Group, 120 Enterprise Avenue, Secaucus,
N.J. 07094

Manufactured in the United States of America
10 9 8 7 6 5 4 3 2 1

Library of Congress Cataloging-in-Publication Data
Fulton, Eileen.
    As my world still turns : The uncensored memoirs of America's soap
opera queen
    by Eileen Fulton with Desmond Atholl and Michael Cherkinian.
        p.    cm.
    "A Birch Lane Press book."
    ISBN 1-55972-274-6
    1. Fulton, Eileen. 2. Television actors and actresses—United
States—Biography. 3. As the World Turns (Television program)
I. Atholl, Desmond. II. Cherkinian, Michael. III. Title.
PN2287.F8A3  1995
791.45′028′092—dc20
    [B]                                                    94-44286
                                                              CIP

# DEDICATION ～

$\mathcal{T}$o Mother and Daddy for their encouragement, not to mention all the bruised thumbs my daddy suffered when he built stages for me to emote upon, and the long hours my mother spent creating beautiful gossamer gowns for me to wear in my "shows." Most of all I am grateful for their indomitable faith in God and, of course, their children.

My darling brothers, Jimmy and Charles, who have laughed and suffered with me through divorces No.1, No.2, and No.3— plus a few loves here and there—and were always there to pick up the pieces (literally and figuratively) as I moved from apartment to apartment and house to house from coast to coast.

My dearest friends, Miss Frankie, David Granoff, Kenneth Muldoon, and Melissa Goldsmith, who have encouraged, listened and, on occasion, held my hand when I was sick.

My deepest thanks to Desmond Atholl and Michael Cherkinian for the many hours they spent listening to my saga with great compassion, love, and many cups of freshly brewed tea.

I am ever grateful to my television show, *As the World Turns,* my sponsor Proctor & Gamble, and my literary agent at William Morris, Mel Berger. Many thanks to my editor Hillel Black and Carol Publishing, my attorney Marc Jacobson, and business advisors Ed Weisel and Nat Silver.

And, of course, the many wonderful fans who have watched my world turn both onscreen and off for the past thirty-five years.

# Contents ∼

# Prologue ～

*E*veryone has what I call "a defining moment" in life: the instant in which suddenly all of the puzzle pieces fit together, and you can finally see the picture you've been working so hard to create.

If you're a lawyer, it might be that first day on the job straight out of law school: You nod approvingly at the beautifully engraved name plate on the office door, line up the diplomas your mother paid a small fortune to have framed, slowly sink into the seat of a fine leather chair, and think "Yes! Yes! Yes! Success at last!" Or if you're the proud mother of an adorable five-year-old girl, it could be that first day of kindergarten: You dress your daughter in a perfectly matched ensemble of pink-and-white, blow her a kiss good-bye as she runs to join one of her neighborhood friends, and then leave the school yard with a lump in your throat but a smile on your face, knowing you've done everything possible to prepare your child to make her way in the world.

But if you've always wanted to be an actress and your sights were set on becoming the first deliciously wicked, scheming vixen on daytime television, what could possibly be a more definitive measure of success than having total strangers call you a "bitch" and a "whore" or having your ears boxed on the streets of New York.

In 1960, soon after I began my life as Lisa Miller on *As the World Turns,* I started playing scenes with Ronnie Welch (my first Bob Hughes). Necking with him, seducing him, trying *any-thing* to snare the boy, I was definitely a woman with a matrimo-nial mission. It wasn't long before viewers started calling in and sending telegrams from all over the country, declaring, "If that bitch Lisa marries Bob I'll never watch your show again. I can't stand that conniving little tramp. She's wrong for the Hughes family. Stop her!!" Ted Corday, our producer at the time, de-clared, "That's it! You're a hit! You'll be married to Bob in two weeks!!"

A few weeks later I was at Orbach's (a long-gone Manhattan department store) rummaging through a pile of gloves that were on sale. New Yorkers are well-known for their bargain-hunting abilities. Although I'm a girl from the South, I can get as excited about uncovering a bargain as a pig is discovering his first truffle. My fingers probed through the piles in search of low-priced treasures. The moment they brushed against what felt like lush, soft suede, quivering appendages transformed themselves into killer tentacles clinging to their prey. Unfortunately, I was not hunting alone: Another woman seized my discovery at the exact same moment. Both of us stood our shopping ground for what seemed like minutes, unwilling to relinquish the prize. Finally, my opponent threw her hands up in the air and shouted, "You're just like the *bitch* you are on that television show!"

Based on that encounter I knew I was making an impact, but I still didn't feel that I had "made it." I envisioned that moment when I would walk down Fifth Avenue or eat in an elegant restaurant and an excited and adoring fan would ask for my au-tograph. I knew *that* would be my defining moment. I had even prepared for the special occasion by purchasing a fine silver pen with my initials inscribed on it from Tiffany's.

A few days after my glove-wrestling match at Orbach's, I stood in front of Lord & Taylor's on Fifth. A very refined woman approached me, dressed in a pale pink Chanel suit. My instincts told me, "This is it." I was convinced the stylish shopper was going to ask for what would be my first autograph.

"Excuse me, aren't you Lisa on the soap?" she politely inquired.

I thought to myself, *I really am taking off now, I really am being recognized.*

"Yes, I'm Lisa, that's the part I play," I proudly replied as I opened my purse to retrieve the pen.

"Well, I hate you!!" she growled. To ensure I understood the intensity of her feelings, she began smacking me on the arm, knocking the pen out of my hand. Her attack threw me off balance and I tripped into the gutter while a crowd of onlookers nodded in approval. My first reaction was to cry, but as I retrieved my pen and watched that pale pink suit slowly fade into the crowd, I thought, *Wow! You must be doing something right!*

Standing in the gutter in front of Lord & Taylor's that day, I never would have dreamt that thirty-five years later I would still be playing Lisa and I would still be encountering a collection of spirited fans wherever I went. Lisa has become a part of my life—like a close friend or a sister. She's seen me through three husbands, numerous boyfriends, live television, and the death of my father. And I have supported her through six marriages, fifty-two lovers, three children, and one "phantom fetus"—not to mention madness and menopause. Between the two of us, we've racked up more matrimonial miles than Elizabeth Taylor and Zsa Zsa Gabor combined. While we've both had our share of ups and downs, we've always managed to come through smiling, looking forward to the next twist or turn in our story line— the next plot complication.

What follows is a collection of anecdotes, observations, and recollections about our combined experiences. As you'll soon discover, it's been quite a roller coaster of adventure. I can only hope that as my world continues to turn (both on screen and off), the ride will be half as much fun.

# AS MY
# WORLD
# STILL
# TURNS

# ONE

# The Minister's Daughter

$\mathcal{P}$eople often wonder whether being born a minister's daughter influenced my professional life. Was Lisa so bad because little Margaret Elizabeth McLarty (my real name) had to be so good?

If genes or environmental influence have any impact on a person's career path, I was more likely to become a school-teacher than an actress: My daddy, grandfather, and uncle were Methodist ministers, my mother and maternal grandmother were both schoolteachers—and I was never allowed to forget it. It's not that my parents were stuffy or straight-laced, it's just that being the minister's daughter—for the entire congregation to scrutinize—I always had to be perfect. No easy task, especially when you're young.

In certain respects, a minister's life is like an actor's: It's never his own. By the time I was seventeen, we had moved nine times. Every September my daddy attended the Western North Carolina Methodist Conference, which was when the district superintendent determined who was to remain and who was to be moved to another church—sort of like being a contract player in the old days of Hollywood and finding out if your option was being renewed or if you were going to be traded to another studio.

Having a family certainly increased one's value in the Methodist "studio" system. When I was born in 1933 (you can either pull out your pocket calculators or do the math on your fingers to figure out my age), my parents had been married six years, so I was a most welcomed child. My debut took place at Mission Hospital in Asheville, North Carolina. It wasn't long before I became the "star" of the Glenns (my mother's family) and the McLartys because I was the first grandchild: the sole attraction. I loved being the center of attention then and I've been loving it ever since.

My first semiprofessional debut occurred at the age of two in my daddy's church. It was on a Good Friday. The congregation was dressed in shades of grey and black. When they started singing "A Fountain Filled With Blood" I decided they needed some cheering up. I leapt up on the alter and broke into a rousing rendition of "Shortnin' Bread." My father gave my mother a stern look and quietly whispered, "Mrs. McLarty, come get your child." When I finished my song and bowed, the crowd burst into applause, which frightened me to the point of screaming. I had never heard anyone clap in church before. To the ears of a little girl, it sounded like a nasty form of punishment.

"They're spanking me," I sputtered between sobs.

Daddy laughed and the congregation took their cue from him and joined in on the fun, while Mother bounced me on her knee, explaining that this is what people do when they like your performance. It was a lesson I took straight to heart—and never forgot.

In addition to performing, I loved to play dress-up. My mother had discovered that it was a wonderful way to keep me occupied. One day I put on a beautiful lace nightgown of Mother's and went next door to visit Mrs. Fedder. I knocked and knocked. When Mrs. Fedder finally opened the door, she was not amused.

"Oh, my goodness, you precocious little child, go home and get dressed."

"But I *am* dressed, Mrs. Fedder. I've come for tea."

"It's indecent to go parading around the neighborhood like that. You can't have tea with me until you put on some clothes."

My temper was rising. How dare she criticize my sense of style. "This is my evening dress, as anyone can plainly see, Mrs. Fedder!"

She wouldn't budge. Mrs. Fedder grabbed one of the flowered handkerchiefs she kept tucked in her apron pocket and began shooing me away like a pesky fly.

I ran home and had a delightful tea with my mother instead. She assured me that my afternoon ensemble was "absolutely lovely." Playing dress-up developed into one of my favorite pastimes—one I eventually turned into a vocation and continue to enjoy even today.

Mother always set an example for me when it came to taking care of my hair or my skin. Like most children, I adored her and tried to imitate everything she did. One time, however, it cost her dearly. Mother had long, beautiful brown hair. Although our family lived on a very modest budget and she could afford to have her hair done only once a month, she was always perfectly coifed. I used to love to sit in front of the mirror next to her, imagining the day when my curls would grow into a long, luxurious mane.

Mother took great pride in her skin and saved her pennies so she could afford to buy a special cold cream she used to wash her face each day. I was never allowed to play with the cream because it was so costly. One morning, while she was in the kitchen washing dishes, I tiptoed into her bedroom and began inspecting everything on her dresser. I was at that stage where children want to touch and taste everything. I began by opening a little box of pale lavender powder and dipped my tongue into the center of what I thought might be "magic sugar." I soon realized there was nothing magical—or sweet—about the taste of the dry substance. I spilled the powder on the floor.

I next moved two face cloths and discovered the jar of face cream. I began giggling with delight because I knew that my fingers and tongue were only seconds away from indulging one of their greatest fantasies. I carefully twisted the lid off and brushed my index finger across the surface of the cream. Its cool touch and creamy texture convinced me that it must be the next best thing to ice cream. I brushed a bit on the tip of my tongue. Delicious! I was in heaven!!

As I was running my finger around the jar, getting the last of it, Mother walked in. She saw her precious powder sprinkled across the floor and her expensive cream oozing out of the sides of my mouth and began to cry. That was the first time I ever hurt her and I felt awful. Of course, more than just my emotions were involved. I thought I was going to be sick, so I burst into tears. Mother was very understanding about my "experimentation." Although I knew I had hurt her feelings and promised never to play with her cream again, I nevertheless continued my exploration of cleansing products: from cold cream I went on to Ivory soap.

One day, just after my "ice cream" feast, the telephone rang as Mother was giving me a bath. When she returned, she found the bar of Ivory floating in front of me with all four corners bitten off. I started to say something because I knew she *knew,* but when I opened my mouth to defend myself, soap bubbles popped out. My throat was killing me, but I couldn't cry because each time I opened my mouth, the bubbles would appear. I knew it was only a matter of minutes before a lot more than bubbles would emerge. Mother was afraid I was going to die, but as soon as I coughed up the soap particles I felt better.

Perhaps, considering my eventual profession, it was prophetic that I became a "soap addict" at such a young age. I have to admit here and now, though, for the first time—and I know Proctor & Gamble will understand—that I cannot look at a bar of Ivory without feeling slightly queasy because my memory of that experience is so strong.

My desire to become an actress crystallized when my parents took me to see a Sonja Henie movie. It was *One in a Million*—and I remember making up my mind then and there that I was going to Hollywood to be a star like Sonja. The next morning I got out of bed just as the sun was peeking through the lavender bedroom curtains. I packed all of my fancy dresses in my doll's suitcase, bid a silent farewell to the sleeping house, and tiptoed out. When my parents woke and found me gone, they scouted around the house and the yard but found no trace of "Sweetie," my mother's nickname for me. Panic-stricken, they called the police. It wasn't long before the entire neighborhood was on the lookout for the latest "Hollywood Hopeful." Hours later, that afternoon, they found me happily strolling along a street. Of course, my parents were overjoyed.

"Where were you going, Sweetie?" my mother asked.

"I'm going to Hollywood to be a movie star," I matter-of-factly announced.

They smiled and hugged me and began to explain that "you don't walk to Hollywood, you have to take a plane." Well, I didn't forget that for a long time.

Shortly after my fourth birthday, I decided to put on a show for Mother while she was busy in the kitchen. I had seen many shows at church, so I made footlights out of empty milk bottles and lined them up in front of the kitchen door. I made my entrance, bowed, and waited for Mother to applaud—she was always a very enthusiastic audience.

A few minutes into my song-and-dance routine, I became dizzy and fell over the "footlights." The bottles broke and I cut an artery in my knee. The blood flowed so fast Mother almost fainted. She couldn't stop the bleeding, and she couldn't drive me to the hospital because she had to keep applying fresh compresses to my knee. Mother quickly telephoned Daddy and he came running home. That was the only way he could get there at the time, because he walked the mile to church every day to save money on gas. Times were tough, but I was never made to feel it.

Daddy carried me to the car and sped to the hospital. I remember getting a lot of stitches and waking up to see a crowd of friends and relatives hovering over my bed. What I didn't know at the time was that I almost died.

I was very proud of my scar because it looked like a half moon. I showed it to everyone I met, announcing, "I've got a scar that looks just like the moon in the sky." Children have a remarkable ability to recover from the most traumatic experiences. At the time, I regarded my fall—and the scar it produced—as a sign of hope. I thought that since I wanted to be a movie star and there's always a moon around the stars, my scar was an omen: It became my good luck charm. I still have a habit of touching my "moon" before I walk on stage to perform my nightclub act.

A few years later, when my family moved from Winston-Salem to Mount Holly, I was very excited: Surely Mount Holly must be the halfway mark to Hollywood!?

Soon after we arrived, I gave one of my best performances and told my first really big whopper. Whether you're a five-year-old child or a sixty-year-old woman, everyone needs a friend his or her own age with whom one can share experiences, dreams, and just plain talk. My mother played dress-up with me and indulged my world of make-believe, but she couldn't bridge the generation gap. I had no one my age to talk with, and the longing for a brother or sister became so great that I decided I, alone, would have to make it come true.

One night, just before a church meeting, I devised a plan, went over the dialogue in my head, and proceeded to set the stage. Our parsonage was next door to the church. While Mother was getting dressed, I crept out of the house. As I walked into the entranceway, I greeted all of the church ladies— keeping one eye on the lookout for Mother. I turned on the charm, began smiling at everyone, and put my plan into action.

"Good evening, Mrs. Jones. Mother may not be here to-night."

"Oh, my dear, what's wrong," Mrs. Jones replied.

"Why haven't you heard," I began squealing with delight. "Mother is going to have a baby!"

Church gossip spreads faster than frosting on a freshly baked cake. By morning it was all over Mount Holly that Mrs. McLarty was expecting. I was absolutely positive that it would come true. I thought Mother would get so embarrassed that she would go out and find a seed and give it to Daddy. (I had already learned from my parents that babies come from seeds.) Mother never said a word about what I did. Weeks went by and still no baby.

I decided since Mother would not have a child—I would! I gradually made friends with Russell, a next-door neighbor who was my age. For some strange reason, Russell preferred playing with boys, but I was determined that he would be the father of my child. One day while we were having milk and peanut but-ter cookies, I asked Russell to marry me. He accepted as we put our glasses in the kitchen sink. It was the first time in my life I asked a man to marry me, but it certainly wouldn't be the last.

I ran into the backyard all aflutter and asked Mother if it

would be all right for Russell and me to marry. She smiled and said it was a fine idea. By this time I had been the flower girl in a lot of weddings, so I knew a bride had to have a white gown. Mother gave me one of her white satin slips to wear. We had a lovely ceremony in the garden, with Russell's cat acting as my maid of honor. From that moment on, I introduced Russell to everybody and anybody as my husband.

I knew that mothers and fathers lived together, so the day after my "wedding" I told Mother that Russell was moving in.

"Sweetie! Whatever for?"

"We're married and we have to live together and sleep together so we can plant a seed and have a baby!"

I can only imagine what my mother's expression must have been at the time. She tried to explain that there was a difference about fifteen years long between *my* wedding and a *real* wedding. For once in her life she was stymied. Mother made it very clear that despite the fact that we were married, Russell and I were not going to live—or sleep—together.

I was a determined child, however, and was going to have that baby no matter what. So getting a little bowl from the kitchen, I went around the neighborhood looking for seeds to give to Russell so he could fertilize them. I presented Russell with a whole pocketful of seeds, but not one of them worked. I reasoned, with great compassion for my mother, that this might well account for her difficulty in giving me a baby brother or sister. Some seeds, I concluded, were just plain rotten.

Disheartened and facing the fact that my marriage was a failure—and a bore—I decided the time had come to move on to greater ambitions: Hollywood. Wanting to do the right thing by Russell, I asked him if he wanted to go with me. He said his dad was taking him fishing in a week, so he couldn't accompany me. I decided I had fulfilled my obligations, so I announced that our marriage was over and began my preparations for the big move out West.

On the chosen day, I carefully examined my ever-increasing wardrobe, choosing what would be appropriate for a "star." Most important was Mother's best perfume. I knew that a star must always smell as lovely as she looked. I told Mother I was leaving. She nodded and went on with her sewing—my parents had become accustomed to this routine by now.

I finished packing and went to ask Mrs. Pierce (my best friend in all of Mount Holly who lived across the street) if she wanted to go with me. Mrs. Pierce was a wonderful lady who truly understood me and recognized my need to make-believe. She let me wear all of her fine clothes and jewelry and never complained when I practiced fainting on her feather comforters (I had seen this in a movie and was certain it was a skill I needed to perfect). I loaded the little suitcase onto my tricycle and rode up to my neighbor's front door.

"I'm leaving today, Mrs. Pierce. I'm going to Hollywood to be a star. Do you want to come with me?"

Mrs. Pierce's eyebrows rose in direct proportion to the corners of her mouth as she smiled. "Now, Margaret, that sounds like a wonderful idea. Of course I'd love to come with you."

My heart started skipping faster than Susie Walters, the fastest skipper in all of Mount Holly. I never dreamed Mrs. Pierce would want to go—she had a family to look after. When she said Yes, I nearly died. How would I fit her on my tricycle? Was there room in Hollywood for *two* new stars? I wasn't certain.

"Wait here a moment," Mrs. Pierce chuckled, "and I'll throw a few things together."

I thought and spoke quickly. "I'm so sorry, Mrs. Pierce, but I'm in a hurry. I can't wait. I've got to leave now. Hollywood's waiting. Good-bye!"

As I began peddling double-time down the street, I decided to bid a grand farewell to Ruth, a neighborhood girl who wore banana-shaped barrettes and never believed that I would be a movie star.

"Margaret!" she brayed in her annoyingly nasal voice, "you're not going anywhere. You're making it all up."

"Well," I retorted, "I'll call you from the airport and then you'll believe me." I got on my tricycle, rode around the block a few times, ran back in the house, and called Ruth. I made tapping sounds with a pencil near the phone, because I thought they had a lot of typewriters at airports. "Ruth, I'm calling from the airport to say good-bye, dear. I can hardly hear you over all these typewriters. I'll send you a postcard with my picture on it after I make my first movie. I have to rush to catch my plane now. Bye!"

Years later, when I had made a name for myself on *As the World Turns,* I finally sent Ruth the promised postcard.

Uncle Tokie, my mother's brother, helped to feed my need to create a world of make-believe. He could make anyone smile, and he had the same talent for making things grow. Wherever he went, things sprouted and flourished. Tokie had dark, curly hair and gray-green eyes that reflected your face. He also had a cleft in his chin that constantly fascinated me. I used to sit for hours with my lower lip wrapped around a pencil trying to shape my chin like his. I loved and adored my uncle and imitated him a lot.

We celebrated one particular Christmas at my grandmother's house in Asheville. Uncle Tokie was staying with Nanny and working nearby. One evening everyone went out except for Tokie and me.

"We're going to have a wonderful time!" he announced. "I'm going to teach you a new game." Whenever Tokie visited we would play "Going to Hollywood." But since he had recently returned from a vacation in New York City, he decided we should play "Going to New York."

"It's the most glamorous place in the whole world," he

began as if he were about to cast a spell. "Far more exciting than Hollywood."

That didn't seem possible to me, but I knew if Uncle Tokie said it then it must be so. Tokie knew absolutely everything about New York. Daddy had an electric train set in one of the rooms upstairs, so we went up there and pretended to ride the train to New York.

"Would you like to dine at a wonderful New York restaurant?" he asked after our "train ride."

Of course I could hardly wait. Tokie took all of Nanny's beautiful china, silver, and crystal and taught me how to set a fancy table. He gave me lessons about how a lady is supposed to behave on a date. After we had a "sumptuous meal," Tokie decided we should go on a carriage ride through the city. We sat on a pretty little love seat in my grandmother's front parlor and pretended to ride through Central Park and watch people ice skate. After our journey, Tokie "opened the carriage door" for me and said, "You take my arm because you're a lady and I'm a gentleman."

Tokie and I had the loveliest of times together. Years later, our imagined dinners, carriage rides, and adventures became a part of my daily life in New York.

I was absolutely ecstatic when my daddy became a chaplain in the navy and we moved to Staten Island—a jumping-off place for that great and wonderful world of New York City. I was convinced that my dream, which Uncle Tokie had fostered, was going to come true at last. Mother had a friend in New York, Emily Kalter, who was a contralto with the San Carlos Opera Company at City Center. One Saturday afternoon we went to hear her sing in *La Traviata*. After the performance, everyone was crowding around Emily and congratulating her. I wandered off onto the empty stage, trying to imagine myself as the hero-

ine. I stood center stage, envisioning a packed house—all waiting to see and hear my performance—and began singing pas-
sionately to my fans. Mother found me and as she took my hand
and led me off I said, "Someday, you'll see—I'm going to be a
star."

The next day Mother sat me down and gave me a lecture.
"Sweetie, darling, I'm sorry but the crown must come off. You
have got to stop living in a dream world. You have got to face
reality."

I all but died. Twenty-four hours earlier I had felt like I was
floating through the sky in a beautiful balloon, surveying the
breathtaking countryside. Now someone was trying to let out
the air and sink me back down to the ground. I'm certain my
mother was just trying to protect me from a life of disappointment. At the time, I couldn't understand why she failed to realize that *this was what I wanted*—nothing else would ever be right
for me.

*I'll never take off the crown,* I thought. *From now on I just won't
let you know I'm wearing it.*

A few months after we moved to Staten Island I was introduced
to a friend of my father's, Dr. Victor Berger, who was superintendent of schools on Staten Island. Dr. Berger quickly understood my hunger for the arts. He kindly arranged for me to
attend P.S. 45—instead of the school in my neighborhood—
because they had a drama department. He told me not to let
anyone know where I went to school because it was against the
regulations to attend a school outside of your immediate vicinity. I agreed but it was difficult. The kids on my block must have
thought I had lettuce leaves for brains when I told them I
couldn't remember the name of my school. I eventually told
everyone I attended a private school.

Daddy, not realizing it, gave me my first acting lesson. I was in the fifth grade and had to learn the Preamble to the Constitution of the United States. I was having a terrible time.

"Old girl," he began, "now just think what you're saying. What does this line mean . . . and this word . . . ?" He took it apart bit by bit. Suddenly the Preamble became an acting piece and I had no trouble with it at all. The next day the other students stumbled over the big words but, to me, every inch had been explained, so I breezed through the piece. Knowing the meaning of what you're saying is one of the fundamental principles of acting.

The next year was the happiest for me because Mother was finally going to have a baby—totally without my help this time. Jimmy was on his way. Mother was having a tough time with the pregnancy and had to go to the hospital because it looked like she might have a miscarriage. After a few days, the danger passed and she seemed to be all right. Since Daddy was being shipped out soon, Mother decided we had better go back to Asheville until the baby came. The day Jimmy was born, they called me at school to tell me I had a baby brother. I ran back into the classroom and was so excited I yelled, "I'm a brother!" My teacher, Mrs. Minerva, made me stay after school because I made myself "obscene" by calling myself a brother. Mrs. Minerva always had it in for me.

Daddy finally got out of the navy. After a short stint back in Staten Island, we moved to Marion, North Carolina. The church in Marion was some distance away from our new home, which was quite different from the modest but livable parsonages in which I had grown up. This was a big, ugly old house and badly needed a lot more than paint. Now that I look back on it, I realize it had many distinguishing features that I couldn't appreciate at the age of fourteen. The woodwork was beautiful.

A slender, handsome spiral staircase dominated the enormous hall. The ceilings were sky high, and the floors were of deep mahogany.

Even though I was told this Victorian house had once been the center of attraction in all of Marion, it still stood like some old horror movie setting to me. I expected Bela Lugosi to say I was sleeping in his bed or to find the Headless Horseman galloping through the long hall. I was scared out of my mind to live in that house. After a few weeks, I really worked on liking the monstrosity, because I realized I had no choice: I might as well make the most of it. I retreated into my world of make-believe. After a few weeks of brainwashing myself, with the help of an over-eager imagination, I finally came to like it.

It wasn't long before the parsonage became a Southern plantation. I would run upstairs when I came home from school and act out the days of Scarlett O'Hara. I had a lot of evening dresses, some Mother's and some she had made for me. I would put on one of the pretty creations and pretend to entertain a room full of distinguished ladies and gentleman callers.

When I finally got to know the girls at school well enough to invite them over to play my game, they thought I was crazy at my age to want to play make-believe. They just wanted to paint their nails and talk about boys. I liked boys, too, but whenever I would invite them over and put them into my elaborately created romantic situations, they usually bid a hasty retreat.

The most thrilling moment of our lives came when we were told that our church was going to build us a house. They hired the finest architects in North Carolina and, for once, we had something to say about what we wanted. Watching the beautiful house go up gave me a feeling of truly belonging to something. That house was ours. Mother was deliriously happy because for the first time in her married life, she could select the kind of furniture she liked and the color schemes she wanted.

A year after we moved into our new home, my younger brother Charles was born. The first day Mother got an attack of morning sickness, I was downstairs with little Jimmy. I heard her and thought, *Oh, no. Another baby to take care of.* It wasn't that I didn't love Jimmy or had ever been jealous of him. On the contrary, I adored him. I had waited a long time for my brother and tending to him was like being a mother.

It's just that I felt deprived of the freedom other children had. I wanted to be popular and have loads of dates and go to the drugstore every afternoon after school like they did. I wanted to sip Cokes and flirt. When you are very young, you don't always understand your responsibilities. Believe me, I knew by then that I was the *minister's* daughter and could not do all the things the other kids did. But that didn't stop me from wishing.

I was dying to smoke. I wanted to smooch and swear like everyone else, but I knew I couldn't. I owed my daddy that respect. I couldn't say "hell" and I couldn't say "damn," but damned if I didn't want to. I was confused by my emotions and began to feel guilty. I wasn't supposed to think that way or act like other kids because it could hurt Daddy's reputation. It wasn't that I didn't love my parents, God knows I did. I proved it all of my adolescent life by suppressing my desires and "being good." But I began to think that always "being good" was just plain horrible.

I continued to write little plays and songs as an escape from my "good girl" existence, auditioning for parts in the school plays whenever the opportunity arose. I thought that if I could just merge my make-believe world with the real one, I'd be fine. One autumn, I auditioned for the lead in a play called *Sunny of Sunnyside.* I wanted the part of Sunny so badly I couldn't sleep nights.

Eva, a girl who had always treated me kindly and whom I

considered a friend, was awarded the lead. I was devastated. The moment I heard the news, I was certain Eva would surrender the part to me—surely she understood that I wanted the lead a thousand times more than she did. Of course she didn't.

One day during a rehearsal, some smart aleck snapped, "You're no different on stage than off. You're so dramatic you make us sick. What's the matter with you?!"

I was confused and taken aback. "I don't know," I sputtered. "I'm an actress!" I could not understand why I should be different on a stage. To me, there was no separating the two.

The following summer, in 1946, Daddy told us we were moving to West Asheville in September. We had lived four years in Marion (quite a long run for a Methodist preacher), and even though I had been an outcast much of the time, I felt sad about going. Living in West Asheville, however, meant being near my Grandmother, Uncle Tokie, and other members of our family whom I dearly loved, and that was some compensation. I was now going to be a senior in high school. Moving is a problem for any young person, even if you're accustomed to it. It means proving yourself and trying to be accepted. This was especially difficult for me, because I always felt different and out of sync with the other kids.

I was a pretty girl, not beautiful, but pretty—so I became an immediate threat to all the girls. They wasted no time in staking their claims to boyfriends and made it quite clear that I was welcome to the leftovers. Not having any close friends, or even acquaintances, only intensified my desire to find an outlet in which to express myself. I became active in the drama group and glee club. This was the loneliest time of all because I was seventeen. I wanted lots of boyfriends because I was convinced marriage was out there just waiting for me. I didn't think about how I would juggle both a husband and a career—quite prophetic, considering my subsequent track record. I just wanted to be popular with the boys.

It took a few months, but the gods of adolescent romance finally answered my prayers. I got a boyfriend named Jimmy who took me to movies and dances. Unfortunately, it didn't last long. Back then, the fad was to keep your supplies in your boyfriend's locker. One day I went to meet Jimmy between classes to pick up some books. He opened his locker with the meanest bang and threw my books on the floor, yelling, "Here you go. Now stay away from me, you slut!"

Jimmy was such a nice boy and I had never seen him angry. I knew the word "slut" was bad because of the way he said it, but I was unfamiliar with the term, so I couldn't quite figure out why he was angry. Jimmy slammed the locker without further explanation and stomped off.

I stood there bewildered by his actions. As I was trying to figure out what had happened, I noticed that all the kids were snubbing me as they passed by. Not one person would speak to me. The boys were looking me over with a nasty gleam in their eyes. Finally, I grabbed Lewis, a boy who had once been nice to me.

"Lewis, please, what's wrong? Why are people acting like this? What have I done?"

He jerked his arm away and sneered at me as if I had just murdered my parents. "We know that you do it with everybody—"

"I do what?!" I interrupted.

"I can't be caught talking to you . . ." he mumbled as he began to run away.

I grabbed him with an uncontrollable force. "No! Wait! Tell me. I DO WHAT?!!"

"Look," he whispered, "you should know what you *do* and what you don't *do.*"

Whoever thought a little two letter word could inflict such pain. I felt nauseated as he walked away, certain the end of the world had been announced. When you're young everything has a life-and-death importance. Having something as important as my reputation attacked so viciously was devastating. Somebody—no doubt a jealous girl—had started this horrible lie about me. It was so unfair because I didn't even pet in those days. The thought that I was doing the "Big I-T" was too ridiculous for words. I had behaved properly all my life and never did anything to harm my daddy's reputation.

My mind began racing out of control. What if Daddy got kicked out of the church because of his "wayward daughter who had become a slut." By the time the gossip reached him, no doubt, I would be expecting twins with the letters "P-W-T" (Poor White Trash) permanently imprinted on my forehead. Fear quickly turned to fury as I realized I was being condemned for something I hadn't even had the pleasure of knowing or doing.

I marched straight into the dean of women's office to straighten out the horrible lie. The dean was extremely busy, but I insisted she listen. After all, this was *my* life everybody was destroying. When I finished, she said, "Margaret, the only thing you can do is simply go ahead and do your work. Do what you have to do, and ignore them until it all dies down." She hugged me. "You'll see, it will be forgotten in no time." It was, but that day left quite a scar at the time. Looking back on it now, I realize it was a great piece of advice. Whenever a gossip column or tabloid newspaper prints something about me I don't like, the dean's words still echo in my head: "Simply go ahead and do your work."

I tried to lose myself in the activities of the drama group, attending festivals, participating in outdoor pageants and summer theaters. As soon as I graduated, I enrolled as a voice major at Greensboro College, my mother's alma mater. My days and nights were filled with scholastic studies and theatrical rehearsals.

I felt all of the hard work had finally paid off when, during my senior year, I won the best actress award for two different roles: Prossy in Shaw's *Candida;* and Golux and an elf in Thurber's *Thirteen Clocks.*

Playing Prossy was especially meaningful to me. I got great reviews and after Daddy came to see me perform he proudly stated, "Old girl, you really were marvelous. I can't get over how good you were. You're quite an actress!" That was the first real compliment I had received from him about my acting. His words of encouragement lifted me up into the sky. I floated around on a cloud for weeks.

My performance in *Thirteen Clocks* eventually led to my move to New York City. During a children's matinee of the Thurber play, there was a sudden electrical storm and all the lights went out. The children began to scream, terrified by the storm and the darkness. I don't know where I got the idea, or what made me do it, but staying in character as the elf I began talking to the kids, calming them, explaining that this was part of the show—the evil spirits had turned out the lights. It wasn't long before they were singing camp songs, laughing, and having fun. Local television and nationwide newspaper reporters came to see me. They took pictures and wrote up a story. That was my first big splash of publicity.

When the production closed, my drama teacher, Dr. Parker, invited me to attend a lecture being given by Mr. Norris Houghton, an authority on Stanislavsky. I didn't know who Stanislavsky was—I thought he was probably some relative of Stravinsky and wondered why Dr. Parker wanted me to attend a lecture on a composer. When Mr. Houghton began speaking about the great acting teacher he had known so well, however, everything became clear. With each word he spoke, my passion mounted. I found myself thinking, *Yes, yes, that's the way it is. That's the way to approach acting.* Suddenly I realized I had been clenching my palms and the blood was running out of my hands.

The lecture ended and people clapped politely, but I was savage to get to him. I shoved and kicked my way through the crowd and ran to Mr. Houghton with my hands outstretched. "Please, help me, I've *got* to be an actress!" He was taken aback, as anyone would be to see this crazy-eyed girl standing there, tears pouring down her cheeks.

"God help you," he said as he shook his head.

"Yes," I concurred, "with or without His help I'm going to be an actress. Please. Help me."

He took my face gently into his hands, smiled, and said, "All right. First, you must study. You must go to The Neighborhood Playhouse in New York and study with Sandy Meisner. If you can't get accepted, get in touch with me, and I will help you."

Without telling my parents, I arranged for an interview at the Playhouse and was accepted. A few weeks later I had my first professional job performing in the *Lost Colony* pageant in Manteo, Roanoke Island, off North Carolina. I got small parts in all the mass scenes, screaming, hysterical scenes. The company started calling me Little Sarah Bernhardt because in every performance I would cry real tears. By the end of the summer, I had won the lead in an opera as a Salem witch.

With a new-found confidence and commitment, I returned home from my summer job, marched into the house, and announced, "I'm going to New York to study acting. I've already applied and been accepted to The Neighborhood Playhouse." My tone of voice was clear, calm, and rational, which made it appear as if this was the only course of action for me. It was.

My parents stood there, helpless, because they knew this was not an impulsive decision. It had been the driving force behind all my actions. For the first time in my life, they surrendered me to myself that night. Even with all the plays I had been in during college, and all the positive write-ups I had received in the papers, my parents simply thought it was a nice hobby. To them acting didn't have the substance or meaning of being a school teacher with a monthly salary. To act was to live in a dangerous bubble. They couldn't understand that some people can't live rooted to a desk or a pulpit or in a rocking chair feeding babies. But I went with their blessings, prayers, and long-saved money.

On the day I left home for my "city of dreams," Mother stood in the doorway of the parsonage, looking much smaller than I had ever noticed before. I felt like I was watching her through the wrong end of a pair of binoculars. Although we were only a few feet apart, Mother, the porch, and my childhood seemed miles away. It was frightening and exhilarating all at the same time.

I gave her one last hug and a kiss. As Mother waved goodbye, a river of tears ran down her cheeks. I had finally cut the cord, and although the pain was great for both of us, we both knew I had to go.

I had to pursue *my* dreams.

I had to begin *my* life.

# TWO

# No Obscene Work, Please

*J*ust before my twenty-second birthday in September of 1956, Daddy drove me to New York—that gigantic electromagnetic force field that continues to attract aspiring artists from all over the world. The only thing I could think of during the entire ride was that soon my feet would be walking the pavements of the city I had fallen in love with the first time Tokie had described it to me. With every mile we moved forward, North Carolina faded further back into my memory. My two kid brothers sat eagle-eyed in the back seat looking at the scenery, not feeling my excitement and appearing a bit down in the dumps because I would no longer be around to play half sister, half mother.

It was twilight when we approached Manhattan. As the car crawled along the asphalt carpet that led to my future, I watched the rising sun begin to change the city's color and mood. I could barely contain myself. This "ugly" city without form or symmetry—jammed together like the work of a pair of clumsy child's hands—was mine for the taking! I sat hypnotized by the passing cars, buses, trucks, buildings, and streets that would all become a part of my daily life. I wanted to jump out of the car and touch everything I saw.

Daddy had arranged for me to live at the Alma Mathews Home for Immigrant Girls on Eleventh Street in the Village. He, and Mother, felt relieved that I would be under the protective care of nice Christian ladies. My father and my two younger brothers stayed at the YMCA for a few days until I settled in and began my classes. We spent our time together doing the typical tourist things: sightseeing, going to museums, churches, and even a Broadway show.

My first day at the Playhouse was spent signing in, finding out where my classes would be, and meeting teachers. I passed a girl in the hall who looked very familiar. We both turned around and started talking. In a matter of minutes we realized that we had been passing each other for years. She was from North Carolina and had gone to the University of North Carolina in Chapel Hill. We had both attended many of the same lectures. While we were comparing notes about some of the more memorable speakers, my new friend suddenly screamed.

"Oh, my God! *Now* I remember you! You're the girl who ran screaming up to Norris Houghton, crying for help about becoming an actress."

Well, who could possibly forget a sight like that. Dasheila and I became good friends from that moment on. I knew my father would be pleased to hear that there was another North Carolina girl attending my school.

That afternoon, while I was waiting for Daddy to pick me up, a man strolled out of the Playhouse wearing an outlandish orange shirt. I hadn't seen him before, so I asked him if he worked there—I thought he might be the janitor because he looked a little scruffy. The gentleman smiled at me and assured me that The Neighborhood Playhouse kept him gainfully employed. I smiled back and said I hoped to see him again.

When my daddy arrived I waved good-bye to the man and hopped in the car. The next day I learned that the "janitor" was

actually Sandy Meisner. I couldn't believe it! I had met God—
and he was wearing an orange shirt!

Two days later, when Daddy packed the car to return home,
I felt sad to part from my family but exhilarated to begin my new
life. Jimmy and Charles stared into my eyes, each asking the big
question: Why?

Daddy looked wisely at me, pipe poised just so in the side of
his mouth, studying me for a moment as if he wanted to take
one last mental photograph. I could always read his kind and
gentle face, and I knew that his silence contained a prayer, wishing me well and the fulfillment of my ambition. A new loneliness crept into the corners of his loving brown eyes. His little girl
had grown up. She had her own world to discover. One beyond
the mountains of North Carolina, alien to the McLartys or the
Glenns. As Daddy got in the car, I saw him rub the back of his
hand against his cheek to wipe away a few tears. It was the first
time I had ever seen my father cry.

I threw myself into my new life with a vengeance, studying with
such talented instructors as Sandy Meisner, Martha Graham,
Pearl Lang, Yuriko, Bob Ballard, and Jane Dudley. I realized it
was important for me to take voice lessons, so I got permission
from the school to work a part-time job to pay for an independent instructor. My definition of part-time, however, was quite
different from theirs. On Monday and Thursday nights and all
day Saturdays, I sold hats at Macy's. I squeezed in another job
singing for the Union Theological Seminary on Sundays, with a
Wednesday night choir practice, and worked out an arrangement where I gave speeches at the Woman's Society of Christian Service to help pay for my rent at the Alma Mathews
Home. It was a tight schedule but I loved it. When you pour all
of your time and energy into creating something you want—
something you believe in—you find you can survive on little
sleep and food. I felt lucky to be given such a chance.

While I was living at the Alma Mathews Home I needed to find a place to practice my voice lessons. They wouldn't let me run through my scales and arpeggios because they thought it annoyed the other residents. Never one to be deterred by an obstacle, I located a nearby Methodist church that gave me permission to use one of their Sunday school rooms. One particular morning I had just started warming up when the head of the church choir knocked on the door and shooed me out. She said another singer had reserved the room to rehearse for an upcoming church performance.

"I can't believe it!" I cried. "I always rehearse at this time. Who have you given my slot to."

"Miss Leontyne Price," the directress announced. (This was well before Ms. Price had made a name for herself.)

I remember thinking at the time, "Who in the land of Jesus has a name like that! And who does she think she is taking my room and my time." Years later when I heard her sing, I thought, "Now I know why they asked me to leave that day."

There was a charming young man at the Playhouse to whom I was very attracted. Bill was blond and blue-eyed, and he came from the South. He made me feel safe and warm. One Saturday night he met me at Macy's and we went to a diner for a hamburger. When I confided to Bill about all of my part-time jobs, he studied me for a moment just like my daddy used to do—his forehead creased in worry lines, and his eyes filled with compassion. Bill slowly took my hands and held them.

"I really admire you," he confessed. "I wish I had your drive, but please don't make yourself sick. Will you promise you'll take good care of yourself?"

He was so kind and gentle. I was genuinely touched by his concern. It was his kindness that led me to make the mistake of marrying him. And it was his concern for my well-being that led him to make the mistake of asking me. We were good friends, and we should have kept our relationship on that basis. When you are very young, however, love seems as important as life itself. To love someone and to be loved by them is the most wonderful thing in the world, but our marriage was impulsive. There's a big difference.

About two weeks after classes began, a group of students decided to organize an evening scene-study class in which we could rehearse with our acting partners in front of each other. The meeting place was in a very undesirable part of town, but I didn't know it at the time. This particular area had such a bad reputation that cabdrivers didn't even want to drive through its crime-infested streets.

I had forgotten the exact address, so when I got out of the subway I started trying to remember the way. I had been to the apartment once before, and I thought I would recognize the building, but the brownstones all looked alike. It was evening and the street wasn't bustling with the same activity I remembered from when I had been there during the day. Shadows of staggering bums appeared from time to time, and, more than once, I had to step over the bodies of poor souls who had made their bed on the sidewalk. Not knowing the address, I started going in and out of all the buildings looking at the names on the mailboxes.

Not having any luck, I saw a store on the corner. I walked in and asked the cashier if he knew where Joyce lived. The gentleman didn't speak English and began rattling away in Spanish as if I had done something wrong. I ran out of the store, found a dime in my pocket, and telephoned Joyce—thanking God that I remembered her number. When she asked me where I was, I couldn't tell her. I was so lost I had no idea. I didn't know the name of the store, so Bill got on the phone and asked me to describe where I had been and the store I had visited. Fortunately he recognized my location from the description and came and rescued me. When he told me how dangerous the neighborhood was, I almost threw up.

That night, I was working on a scene with a boy named Charles. The material was very dramatic. I took the character I was portraying quite seriously, and fueled by my anxiety from being lost, I got caught up in the moment and slugged my acting partner. Out of reflex, Charles hit me back. Everybody was shocked. So was I. I snatched my coat and flew out the door. Bill came chasing after me. I'd never been hit by a boy before. We were both young actors who had lost control of the moment.

While Bill and I were on the way home, poor Charles called the boarding house to apologize. He spoke to Miss Hovell and she told him I wasn't in.

"Well, Miss Hovell," Charles had said, "when Maggie returns tell her I hope I didn't hurt her when I punched her."

Of course, my good and faithful Christian guardian hit the ceiling.

When Bill brought me to the door, Miss Hovell was waiting—without her teeth. She cracked open the door and barked, "Ith thith the young man who hit you?"

Bill and I laughed but Miss Hovell didn't see the humor in the situation. She told Bill to leave, escorted me to her room, and—after putting her teeth in—proceeded to lecture me about the evils of the theater. She added I was letting my father down because he was a minister.

"Margaret, the only sensible course is for you to go back home and get married and have lots of babies."

I was so tired that I leaned my head back in the chair and fell asleep right in the middle of her speech. I didn't mean to, but I had worked all day at school and put in four hours at Macy's before attending the group scene study. Miss Hovell woke me up with a hard shake and snapped, "Go to bed and just be glad you're sleeping alone!"

Just before the Christmas break, during my first semester at the Playhouse, the office secretary made an appointment for me with a representative from *Life* magazine. They were doing an article on young women who were the most likely to succeed in their chosen career. I had a week to get ready for this important event, which I was convinced would change my life. I was positive they would select me out of all the actresses as the one who would make it to the top. I wrote my parents to tell them to get ready for my "break." I washed out my black sweater and matching skirt. I had a little white collar and white cuffs to go with it. This was my idea of the young girl who was going to make it.

When the day of the interview arrived, I sat in the office at The Neighborhood Playhouse, looking down at Rockefeller Plaza, being very sure of myself. The interviewer sat listening to the story of my life and began to look increasingly bored. I, of course, was Miss Enthusiasm—the answer to his problem in finding *the* actress. I felt like announcing, "Here I am! You need look no further. Now you can concentrate on finding your lady doctor and lawyer and executive." I tried to charm the pants (figuratively speaking, of course) off the man but he wasn't interested in anything I had to say. It finally ended by him asking, "Uhh, what did you say your name is?" It was my first big disappointment but certainly not my last.

Bill and I had been dating and attending classes together for almost five months. He really went out of his way to take care of me, picking me up after work to make sure I got home safely. There's something about that kind of old-fashioned gentlemanly charm that makes men irresistible to me. We loved to go to the theater together whenever we could afford the tickets. One Valentine's Day—which was also Bill's birthday—I purchased two tickets for *The Iceman Commeth* with Jason Robards. We sat at little tables for the show and afterward Bill said, "Let's go somewhere." I didn't know what he meant at the time. We got into some heavy necking and a few hours later I was no longer a "good girl." The minister's daughter had finally done the dirty deed!

In no time at all Bill proposed. I thought, well, why not? That was probably the only way I could handle what was becoming an increasingly hot affair. Besides, I thought at the time, I should do the honorable thing and marry the boy after I slept with him—make a decent man of him! Deep down I knew I didn't want to get married, but I didn't know any other way to handle what was going on. I thought I loved him. I've since learned that you can love a lot of men, but it doesn't mean you should rush to the nearest church and marry them all.

Our first fight—and the first real signpost signaling "Disaster Ahead"—occurred a few days after he had given me a ring. We were having coffee in a diner and I said dreamily, "Oh, how wonderful the wedding will be. We'll have the biggest wedding in the world and Grandfather McLarty, Daddy, Uncle Emmett, who is also a preacher, will all conduct a grand and elaborate wedding ceremony." I clapped my hands in excitement. "Now, Bill," I continued, "we have to decide what kind of silver and crystal and china we want . . ."

My fiancé slammed his coffee cup on the Formica table, splashing the murky liquid all over my white cotton blouse. "I don't want all that junk!" he screamed, attracting the attention of everyone within a three-block radius. "China, silver, crystal!! I just want you to be my wife."

"But Bill," I persisted, "when you get married everybody gives it to you. All we have to do is tell them what we like . . ."

He jumped up and ran out. I quickly threw some coins on the table and followed him. Bill had an umbrella in his hand (he always carried an umbrella) and when I tried to talk to him, he started beating it against the wall, yelling at me. I was terrified. I had never seen anyone lose control like that. That fight should have told me something, but it was soon forgotten. We set the wedding for July. As the date approached the truth was obvious—we were not well-matched—but neither of us had the courage to say it aloud.

My parents were not entirely enthusiastic at first, but they supported me in my decision to marry. Mother adored Bill when she finally met him. She thought he was a lot like Daddy, the way he took over and managed everything. Bill was wonderful to her—and to my brothers—and I adored him for that. The gown Mother bought me was beautiful. I kept telling myself over and over that this was going to be the happiest day of my life, trying to brainwash myself the way I did about that spooky house in Marion. But the more I thought about it, the more frightened I became. I felt as if I was going to my own funeral.

We got married in my daddy's church and had a quick honeymoon in Florida. Three days later, we returned to New York and stayed in an inexpensive hotel while Bill began looking for an apartment. One day, he staggered in all worn out and grumbled, "All you have to do is lie here and read your scripts and magazines while I trudge all over town, walking my balls off to find you a place to live!"

We were not in a perpetual state of bliss—more like two kids who had gotten in over their heads. A few days later he returned from his search and I told him that I had counted up the remaining money we received from the wedding and decided we could afford a toaster and coffee pot. That set him off like a firecracker on the Fourth of July.

"You can't spend that!" he began screaming. "I need that money and you can't spend it on toasters! I have to pay back my parents."

I didn't know what he meant. He began to confess that he

had gone to the dog races while we were in Florida and lost all the money he had borrowed to set up an apartment. His admission only served to increase the tension between us.

Thankfully, two days later, Bill found a one-room apartment on Ninety-Sixth Street and Central Park West. It was small, in a nice brownstone, and had potential. We both started our second year of classes at the Playhouse. The routine seemed to stabilize our relationship for a while. That year—1957—was a rough one for us. I could stretch a dollar better than the best. My weekly grocery bill never exceeded ten dollars. We didn't mind pinching pennies because we believed fame and fortune were just around the corner.

Bill and I graduated from The Neighborhood Playhouse and began the real work of trying to earn a living as actors. Ours was an elevator marriage: quick "hellos" and a peck on the cheek as we ran in and out of the apartment to jobs, auditions, meetings—anything we thought would bring us closer to our dreams. Bill quickly took a job as a waiter to keep us going. He worked hard and his hours were exhausting, but no matter how much I insisted on going back to a sales job, he refused: "You're supposed to be an actress. I'll make the money and you get a job performing. You're too talented to work in a damn store anyway!"

I started pounding the pavement in the early morning looking for modeling jobs, auditioning for plays, and trying to see agents. Bill's job waiting tables started at 5 P.M., which was about the time I usually dragged myself in the door after a day of rejections. He didn't return until 3 A.M., so the only time we saw each other was in bed. I didn't want to let days go by like that, so I would set my alarm clock and wake up before he came home. I felt it only right that we should spend a little time together, but my being awake seemed to make him angry. One night when I was waiting for him he yelled, "If I'm going to work myself to death for you, then you'd better get up early and make the rounds, which you can't do if you don't get enough rest!"

My first few jobs were not the sort that win actors Oscars and Tonys. First I modeled preteen-sized clothing in the garment district but was fired the next day because I was too "busty" for a preteen. Next I got an assignment for *True Story*, the confession magazine. I made it clear that I wouldn't do any obscene work. "No bra and panty scenes, no nightgowns. Nothing less than a slip." The experience was not the most rewarding artistically, but I earned one hundred dollars for a few hours of work—a fortune when you're counting pennies.

The world of modeling, however—especially the level at which I was working—was hardly glamorous. It was crawling with strange, seedy, styleless men who tried to take advantage of young impressionables. At least that was my experience then. There was always the inevitable question: "Would you like to make some extra money, honey? I know you're a serious actress, but nudes are very artistic."

Despite my refusals, the men were very persistent. Some of these creeps would bar the door or try to con me into staying. Others would grab my bust, thinking their touch would send me into a swoon, no doubt. I elbowed, punched, and kicked more men that year than a Sumo wrestler. Bill and I finally agreed enough was enough. I would just have to concentrate on acting and skip the bread-and-butter modeling money. It wasn't worth the aggravation.

Fortunately, just after we agreed that I should quit modeling, Bill got a part in the Broadway show *The World of Suzie Wong*. I was thrilled that he landed the first acting job because I thought it would ease the ever-increasing tension in our relationship and secure our marriage. Instead, I became jealous of all those gorgeous Oriental girls he worked with. Bill showed me how they gave him an Oriental back rub. The way he talked about them I became convinced he was fooling around. By the time the show previewed on the road, I was very upset. I was tormented by the image of all of those "Suzies" seductively stroking my husband's shoulders.

When my birthday came around on September 13, I waited all day for a present from Bill. Nothing came. No card, no gift, no call. I was very depressed and I had a voice lesson that afternoon, so I went next door to my neighbor's and asked her if she would listen for my doorbell because I was expecting a present. She told me not to worry. Confident the gift would come, I left to keep my voice lesson with Colin Romoff.

For sixty blissful minutes I forgot about Bill and birthdays but the minute it was over I announced, "Colin, today is my birthday."

"Goodness! Really? What special things are you and your husband going to do?"

"Well, he's out of town," I replied, tears welling up in my eyes. I bit my lip and gulped a lot.

"You poor child. How terrible for you."

"It's okay," I stated in a falsely reassuring tone, "my husband won't forget."

I went home and waited. It was still early and I just knew Bill wouldn't let my birthday go by. The phone rang and I raced for it, certain my hero was telephoning with a wonderful birthday wish. It was Dasheila, my friend from North Carolina who had also studied at the Playhouse.

"Maggie, I remembered today is your birthday and I know Bill is out of town. I think we should celebrate. Let's have tea."

Dasheila was very thoughtful and considerate. She brought me a lovely fleur-de-lis pin. I served her tea and after an hour she left.

I washed the cups and saucers and sat by the window hoping to see a mailman bringing a present to me. It was a cold day and the sun was barely breaking through the heavy smog above the city. Later that night I got out the present my parents had sent a few days earlier, which I hadn't yet opened. I stuck a candle in a cupcake and sang "Happy Birthday" to myself. I made a wish (that Bill would send me a present), blew out the candle, opened my presents, and tried to go to sleep. I tossed and turned for hours. By two o'clock that morning I couldn't stand it any longer so I called Bill in Philadelphia. He was out and I panicked. I thought maybe he was ill and that would explain why he hadn't sent me a card or anything. I kept calling back every half hour and finally I fell asleep. About five that morning I got a call from him.

"What the hell have you been calling me for?"

"Today is my birthday, Bill."

"Oh, Lord, Maggie . . . can you forgive me?"

He explained how hard they were working on the show and that night he had gone out with some of the boys. He really felt awful. Two days later I got a card from him with a little housewife on the front pushing a grocery cart! It was not exactly what I had hoped for.

While Bill was out of town for the summer, I set a goal for myself to find an agent before he opened on Broadway in the fall. I was determined to find someone to represent me—even if I had to nail him to the chair to make him listen to me.

One Friday afternoon it was hot as blazes. I'd been knocking on doors all day, but I wouldn't give up. By the time I reached William McCaffrey's office I was a bit wilted, but the sun had recharged my batteries. I knocked on the door and heard voices, but no one answered. I knocked a few more times—still no response. After a few seconds of silence, I heard loud laughter. I could feel the steam beginning to rise out of me like a tea kettle about to explode.

How dare they laugh at me!

Utilizing the Sumo wrestling skills I had acquired during my modeling days, I took a step back and gave the door a swift, hard kick. It just collapsed. Unfortunately, so did I. My body, and pride, fell on the floor while my pictures and resumés flew through the air. I was embarrassed but undeterred. After carefully picking myself up, I glared at the once-laughing but now silent group.

"I'm an actress and I need an agent!" I announced.

Mr. McCaffrey's face stretched into a wide, warm smile of approval. "Little girl, with an entrance like that you've got one!" It was the beginning of my professional career and a long friendship with a wonderful man.

About a month after I signed with Mr. McCaffrey's agency, Caroline Allen, the agent there who handled me, suggested that I change my name. She felt Margaret Elizabeth McLarty would not roll off the tongues of New York's most important directors. Of course I tortured everyone I knew for weeks with every name I could think of. I considered calling myself Amanda Asheton but Caroline didn't see this as an improvement.

"They're just going to call you Mandy and picture some southern belle in a hoop skirt."

I finally chose the last name Fulton—my Uncle Tokie's full name was Casius Fulton Glenn. I wanted to use his name because of the impact he had on my early aspirations. I thought about Leila as a first name—after a favorite aunt. When I telephoned Bill, who was on the road, he suggested I call myself Alene.

"Arlene?" I gasped, "I'm definitely *not* the Arlene type."

"No, stupid!" he snapped. "Eileen."

By then I was sick of the name game. "Okay. All right! It's done!!" When I later showed Bill my new Actor's Equity Card with "Eileen Fulton" printed on the front, he started laughing.

"I didn't say 'Eileen,' I said 'Alene.' Like Aileen MacMahan—the actress.

By then it was too late. The card read "Eileen Fulton" and that's the way it was going to stay!

When Bill returned to New York and his show opened on Broadway, we started looking for a bigger apartment. We agreed that part of our problem might be due to the confining quarters. Being in one room—with only the bathroom as an escape—might be too much togetherness. I should have realized then that even if we had lived in the Taj Mahal, it would have been the same situation, but I wasn't willing to face that fact yet.

Soon after, we moved to a bigger apartment. And soon after that, Bill quit his show. I suppose he was hoping to get a bigger part in another show. When he left, however, he just moped around the apartment.

With an agent representing me, I suddenly had access to better parts in reputable and higher-paying productions. My first real acting job was *Blue Denim* in Mount Kisco, New York. As soon as it closed, I returned to New York and landed a part in the off-Broadway production of *Summer of the Seventeenth Doll,* directed by the late Alan Schneider. My career was on a roll. As is often the case, however, professional success is not necessarily related to personal happiness. My relationship with Bill continued to deteriorate to the point where we rarely saw one another—and when we did, it was far from civil.

One afternoon I was looking through Bill's files because I was feeling nostalgic and wanted to see some of our old honeymoon pictures. He got furious when he found I had been rummaging through his papers and books. After screaming and shouting about not having any privacy, Bill began throwing things around the room and pushing me. I got so mad I picked up a pot from the kitchen and cracked him over the head, shouting, "I wish you were dead!" When the verbal dart hit its target,

I came to my senses: *My God,* I thought. *What's the matter with me? Have I gone crazy?!*

I ran into the bathroom to cool down. After five minutes I knew what to do. I decided I had had enough, so I walked back into the living room, sat in a chair, and told Bill I wanted a divorce. For the first time in a long time we calmly talked through our differences and agreed to an amicable separation.

The next day I knew I had to call Mother before she heard the bad news some other way. I didn't know what kind of response to expect, but she was wonderful—so sweet and sympathetic. None of that, "Can't you try to work it out?" I wasn't the preacher's daughter being held up as an example. She was a mother talking to her only daughter whom she loved.

Thanksgiving Day—less than two years after our wedding—Bill and I legally separated. We met with a lawyer and then went out for dinner to celebrate our separation. He was very polite. Our time together was pleasant despite the circumstances. Bill told me he was on his way to California to see what sort of work he could get on the West Coast. I wished him the best of luck.

"Well, Bill," I began with a bit of a lump in my throat, "I hope that Los Angeles brings you loads of personal and professional happiness." I really meant it. I harbored no ill feelings toward Bill. We were just two kids who rushed into marriage and fortunately found our way out before it was too late.

I had a show to do, so we parted outside the restaurant. Bill kissed my cheek, took a step back, and just stared at me in silence the way Daddy did when he said good-bye to me that first time in New York. After a few seconds, his beautiful blue eyes twinkled and his lips curled up into a melancholic smile. "Break a leg, Maggie. Bye."

As we walked away in opposite directions, a great sense of loneliness settled over me. Bill was going far away to that place I had dreamt of as a child. I quickened my pace, thinking that the sooner I walked through the theater's stage door, the sooner I would get on with my life. Sitting in front of the mirror, applying my makeup, I began to feel alive again. I examined the reflection of this twenty-five-year-old woman named Eileen Fulton who stared back at me: She appeared confident, secure, and convinced that something wonderful was right around the corner. I was ready to begin again.

Ask any actor who has an agent and he'll assure you that having one doesn't mean everything magically falls into place. With each audition, I realized I would have to fight for the roles I wanted as fiercely as I fought for my agent. As soon as *Summer of the Seventeenth Doll* closed, I had an interview for a Broadway show called *One for the Dame*. The day I auditioned—before I read—I went up to meet the producer, director, and writer. This was well before the age of casting directors. The three of them looked me over and said, "Thank you very much, leave your pictures here."

"When will you be reading me?" I asked.

"There won't be a reading," they replied. "You're not quite what we're looking for."

I almost started to cry. My first Broadway audition and they weren't even going to read me! "Why?"

"We're sorry but you're just too pretty for the part."

I wasn't ready to admit defeat. "I can look very homely," I stated in my most persuasive voice. Frantically, to convince them I meant what I said, I ripped off my false eyelashes, scrubbed off my lipstick, unfastened all of my jewelry, and destroyed my perfectly coifed hair. I transformed myself from being stylish to spinsterish in sixty seconds! "See? See how homely I am? I'm not a pretty girl at all!!"

They were absolutely hysterical and thought my performance earned me the opportunity to read for the part. The next day, after I'd practically memorized the whole script, I asked, "Did you like it? Have I got it?" They all looked at each other for a second and in unison announced, "Yes!" My character was a little girl who played the violin and thought she was pregnant but eventually found out she just had the measles.

When I got the part, I was afraid of looking pretty for fear they would fire me on the spot. I started wearing jeans and old tattered shirts that Bill had left behind. No makeup other than lipstick. And I whacked off my hair.

There were ten men in the show, and since I dressed like a boy, they treated me like one. It bothered me terribly, but I didn't know what else to do. The job meant everything to me and I wasn't going to let anything get in the way of my Broadway debut. Even with all of my determination and fighting spirit, there were some things I couldn't control: The show closed out of town during tryouts in October of 1959.

My tomboyish experience with *One for the Dame* instigated a real rebellion for me. I realized I didn't have to go back to playing the sweet, adorable, feminine flower of the South. I bought a leather jacket and stomped around the neighborhood in sneakers, blue jeans, and a sweat shirt. I told people around the block I was a member of the Hell's Burners—a neighborhood gang. If I had ever come face-to-face with a real Hell's Burner I would have melted on the spot, but I wanted to act tough since I never had the opportunity before.

I started riding the Staten Island Ferry back and forth. I would stay on it for hours and think about what I was going to do with my life, my attitude toward myself and other people I had loved. I was never again going to be what other people wanted me to be. I wanted to know what it was like to do something wild and crazy because I had never done it before.

I smoked cigarettes on the ferry, choking and coughing my

way to Staten Island and back. Having never been to a bar, I sauntered into the crummiest dump I could find. I didn't want to drink, I just wanted to be brave enough to go into a joint like that.

A gruff-looking character approached me from behind the bar. He had what looked like a field of black parsley growing out of the collar of his low-necked T-shirt, but he certainly didn't smell as inviting as any garden I'd been in.

"Yeah, little girl? What'll ya have?" he asked with a kind of a Big-Bad-Wolf sneer.

I was sick of being called a "little girl" and was not about to play Red-Riding-Hood to this overgrown animal. "I would like a drink!"

"You would, huh!" he grunted. "Well let's see . . ." He lingered for a moment, looking me up and down, until he was ready to finish the sentence. ". . . your driver's license."

I showed it to him.

"Okay, kid, what's it gonna be?"

"Orange juice," I politely replied.

His head shot forward like a rooster's. "Whaaatt?!?!"

He had been washing glasses when I ordered, so I said, "Oh, that's all right, you don't have to wash a glass," thinking that was the right answer. I downed the juice in one swallow like a gunslinger in the Old West. After tossing a quarter tip on the counter, I "moseyed on out of the ol' saloon" feeling much better.

It wasn't an experience I would need to repeat. I did it just to prove to myself that I had the necessary courage to be whatever I wanted. I was ready to break the traditional "good girl" chains that had tied me down most of my adolescent life. If I was going to be proper and clean and good, then it had to be because *I* chose to do so and not because it was expected of me.

A few weeks into my new-found tough girl routine, I auditioned for two roles in the same week—both named Lisa. I would eventually be awarded both parts: One was the lead in a Warner Brothers movie *Girl of the Night,* which opened to mixed reviews; the other, a temporary character in a popular television soap called *As the World Turns,* would irrevocably change my life.

# THREE

# The Birth of a Glamorous Vixen

*P*eople often think that an actor's career has a lot to do with being in the right place at the right time. While that may be true, you can't underestimate the importance of the competition *not* being in the right place. There are countless stories about actors who have had to turn down roles—for whatever reasons—and the individual who actually got the part became famous from it. That's what happened to me in the spring of 1960. In the same week I auditioned for both *Girl of the Night* and *As the World Turns.* And I got both auditions the same way.

The casting office of *Girl* had called my agent, Caroline, and requested to see a certain young actress who, fortunately for me, was about to have a baby. Caroline told Warner Brothers the actress wasn't available but that *I* would be perfect for the part. They agreed to see me and an audition was scheduled. I was thrilled: It was a starring role—a hippie call girl from the South—and if I could get a movie, I felt my career would skyrocket.

Two days later, *World* called the McCaffrey office asking for the same pregnant actress, and, once again, Caroline told them about me. As with *Girl,* the character's name was also Lisa. But the Lisa *World* was looking for was a nice, sweet college type.

Having played the Minister's Daughter for so many years, I knew I could handle a part like that.

The audition took place at Benton and Bowles—a large New York advertising agency. When I walked into the reception area, I discovered a room full of girls who looked just like me, preparing to audition for *my* part. Sitting in a room full of actors who are all competing for the same part is like walking through a beautiful green field full of snakes: At first glance everything seems quite pretty and pleasant, but it's not long before you can sense the danger lurking beneath the surface. As long as you step carefully, you'll be just fine, but one wrong move—sit in someone's chair or breathe in such a way as to disturb someone else's "relaxation exercises"—and you're sure to get bit!

I wore a green print shirtwaist dress I had bought especially for the audition, for the staggering price of $7.50. When I got a copy of the script, I decided the important thing was not to give a perfect line reading but to fill out the character with some color and depth. The scene took place in a drugstore. I was supposed to be sipping a soda with a boy named Bob Hughes, whom I hoped to catch as my steady. There was nothing to indicate what type of family Lisa came from, whether she had brothers or sisters, what she wanted out of life—nothing.

During the thirty-minute waiting period, I began to make up a life for her. I decided she was an only child who was loved, adored, and spoiled to death by her father yet disciplined by a stern mother. Then I began to think how those circumstances might affect the character in the scene. Lisa would think, "I'm an only child. I have everything I want. But Bob is somebody very special. He's going to be a doctor and that means position and money. I'm going to get him to be my boyfriend if it's the last thing I do!"

When I went into the audition room, I met Ted Cordey, the executive producer for *World*. We talked for a while about my background—being a preacher's daughter. Ted told me they were looking for a sweet girl who was going to move into the Hughes family and be Bob's sweetheart. Penny was going to be jealous and Nancy was going to like Lisa because she would remind her of her dead daughter. That was the original idea. Of course, it would all change in time. I could tell Ted liked my spunk and spontaneity. He asked me to return the following week to read with Ronnie Welch, the young actor who played Bob Hughes.

By the time the next audition rolled around a few days later, I had invented an entire life for Lisa and her family. I wore the same dress again, because they seemed to like it the first time and I wanted them to remember me in the same way. Ted's assistant took me to a small studio with a camera. I remember feeling more exhilarated than nervous. Although I had never been in a television studio or performed in front of a camera before, there was a feeling of familiarity—of belonging—like I was home. Ronnie and I sat in chairs and pretended to be sitting in a drug-store. I could see Ted in the control room along with the associate producer, Lyle Hill, and some of the big-wigs from the show's sponsor, Proctor & Gamble.

The audition went very well. Afterward I was told they would get in touch with my agent when they had reached a decision. On the way home, the usual postaudition torment began: that torturous process actors put themselves through, reliving everything they did in the audition, second-guessing every choice they made. "Are they going to realize I can do the part? Is my hair the right color? Am I tall enough? Pretty enough? Please, please, please, let me have the part!!" That was probably the most painful week of my career. Waiting for both Lisa roles.

I didn't have to wait long. Three days later, while auditioning for the musical *Take Me Along* with Jackie Gleason and Walter Pidgeon, my agent came rushing up to me.

"You did it!" she screamed. "You've got Lisa on *As the World Turns!!* Won't it be fantastic if you get the movie, too? Now, go out there and get this musical and you'll be a triple-threat!"

I sang five songs for the director before he decided I wasn't right for the part. It didn't matter: I was much too excited about landing Lisa. Getting that break would give me the first real opportunity to show the public what I could do as an actress. I would finally be paid to practice everything I had learned. And if I also got the movie, wouldn't life be just perfect?

Every now and again life is perfect—for about five minutes. Two days later I won the part of Lisa in the movie. I called my family to give them all my good news. Mother was so excited she cried and Daddy, with his usual calm, easy manner, expressed his delight. Even my kid brothers, who used to think soap operas were corny, congratulated me. Later they became my biggest fans and watched the show whenever they could.

The following week I filmed my first episode of *As the World Turns*. I was twenty-seven years old and terrified, but I maintained a cool facade and tried to act as though it was an ordinary experience. As I entered the CBS lobby, a guard sitting at a desk said, "Can I help you?"

I very proudly announced, "I hope you can. I'm Eileen Fulton!" I was certain the mere mention of *World*'s newest cast member would unlock the gates.

"Arlene who?" he asked.

"No, no, Eileen. Eileen Fulton." I could tell he was not about to roll out the red carpet and sound the trumpets. "I'm with *As the World Turns.*"

He pointed to his left, yawned, and began reading a newspaper. "You go to the right and walk down to the end of the hall and up the stairs."

Readjusting the bag on my shoulder—and my slightly bruised ego—I marched forward.

I entered a small rehearsal hall that was empty except for a long table in the middle and chairs all around. Rehearsal started at two thirty and it was just past two when I arrived. I walked to the windows and looked out on a row of brownstone houses, each with a lovely garden. I saw a man sitting on his terrace, drinking coffee and reading. It was the first warm spring day and I looked at him and thought, *How can you sit there so calmly when I'm about to die?* I was afraid they might fire me before they gave me a chance to show them what I knew I was really capable of doing.

Suddenly the door flew open and all these people I had watched on television came bouncing into the room, laughing, telling stories. I froze, staring at Helen Wagner, Don McLaughlin, Ronnie Welch, and Santos Ortega. Everyone was incredibly kind to the "new kid on the block." After a few minutes, Ted Cordey entered and the room grew silent. Ted was sort of the Sandy Meisner of daytime television. When he walked in, it was as if God had suddenly arrived to bless the congregation.

Ted had kind and sometimes funny things to say, but it all went over my head because I was so terrified about the reading. Readings have always frightened me much more than performances have, because once the acting begins I become lost in the character and forget myself—and my nerves. At that moment, I felt as though I was the only person who had ever had a first day with a national television show. Ted knew the other people. He knew what they were like as actors and that they understood the characters they were playing. But I was new to him. I had never done a soap opera before, and I was afraid that during the reading he would think, *Well, I hired her and if I don't like her today I'll fire her.*

When I learned that Helen Wagner, who plays Nancy (Bob's mother) was married to a producer for whom I had auditioned the summer I graduated from the Playhouse, I relaxed a bit. It was a connection to something familiar. I loved Helen immediately. She was very understanding and tried to ease my tension. She told me about her house in the country and her garden and I realized she was not just an actress but a warm, wonderful human being whose interests were very much centered on her husband and her home. Later on, I learned that all of the cast were family people. I couldn't get over the fact that they went to church, belonged to the P.T.A., and were active in so many clubs and organizations outside of their jobs. At that time I couldn't imagine how they could even think of doing anything other than their work at the studio.

Ted finally took out a stopwatch, pushed the button, and pointed at the person who was to open the first act. In live television, everything is timed to the second. You don't have the luxury of going back and trimming a scene that runs too long or stretching out or redoing a scene that is too short. By the end of rehearsal, I was frightened of the live show I had to do at one thirty the following day. My training at the Playhouse taught me to embrace a role slowly, carefully—an approach that would never work in the frenetic, fast-paced world of television.

The next morning, on the way to the studio, waves of nausea flooded over me. My legs began to wobble. I kept vacillating between uncontrollable excitement and total terror. My first scene took place in a drugstore called the Sweet Shop. This was a particularly important meeting place on *World* where the young lovers like Penny and Jeff would meet. It seemed only fitting that Lisa and Bob would have their first date in this romantically old-fashioned locale.

The scene opened with me sipping a soda and talking to Bob Hughes. I took a deep breath and tried to focus on the scene, thinking, *Here I am in the Sweet Shop with Bob—the boy I want to go steady with.* It was as if he were the "Bill of my dreams" and I was going to nail him. Suddenly out of nowhere, organ music swelled in the air and broke my concentration. How could I know that it was the theme music for the opening of the show? I hadn't heard any music during rehearsal. I never even noticed it when I watched the soap at home. I was completely rattled— but that was only the beginning.

The soda tasted like spoiled milk—shaving cream had been substituted for whipped cream on the top. I sat through the whole scene, sipping this slop and acting like it was the greatest drink on earth. The prop men hadn't counted on my swallowing the stuff. They nearly died with laughter. I soon realized I had a lot to learn. When the scene was over, I ran back to my dressing room and tried to calm down. But I was in for one more shock. Don McLaughlin, who played Bob's father, poked his head in the door to see if I was all right.

"My dear," he began, "I saw your scene and I thought you were wonderful, but don't go out and buy your Rolls-Royce yet. If you have what they want to work with, you've got a job, but if you don't, just remember it doesn't mean you aren't good—because I think you are. I just want you to know that. If they don't hire you, it simply means you aren't the type they're looking for."

I thought he was very kind and I appreciated his encouraging words, but what Don didn't know was that no one had mentioned the part *wasn't* mine. I had no idea I was being tested. I later found out that Irna Phillips, the show's creator and writer, had the final say as to whether I would live part of my professional life in Oakdale. Before I left that day, the producer told me a decision would be reached within three weeks.

A few days later, my agent called to say I really did have the part. The following day I signed my contract for the movie. There wasn't a happier actress within a three-thousand-mile radius of New York. Caroline had promised there would be no problems with the two work schedules. What more could I ask for?

I had only been on the show twice and Ted was concerned about the way I gave a cold reading because my timing was off. He wouldn't hesitate to inform me of the fact whenever it happened. He would also stop me on specific lines and give me a line reading (saying the line in a way that I was supposed to imitate). At my third afternoon rehearsal, I blew up and slammed my fist down on the table.

"Damn it, Ted! Please don't give me line readings. You say a line one way because you are a certain person. I could never say it your way because I am a different person. Tell me what you want, but please don't tell me how to say it!"

My feisty spirit and serious approach to acting quickly overrode any fears I may have had about challenging any authority figures.

Ted stared at me with raised eyebrows over the tiny glasses he wore on the end of his nose. Everybody in the room gasped and looked down at their scripts, embarrassed. A few of the men laughed because they liked the spitfire in me.

I knew Ted could fire me at any moment, yet I felt if he understood how I functioned as an actress, we would have a better working relationship. I truly liked and respected him, but he had to understand that I felt it was insulting to be told *exactly* how to say a line. When he eventually began to see what I could do with the part, he became my greatest ally. Ted was responsible for my being given the opportunity to develop Lisa.

One thing that worried me in a TV series of this kind was that you might do only one or two shows a week, and if one show was not quite up to par, you might be off television for the rest of your life. Even the greatest actor in the world can have an off day, but if you're on live television, the pressure to be perfect can be unbearable. Until I learned not to worry about it, the fear stood in my way. I remember getting notes before air, just before we went live, from Ted telling me "this is wrong and that doesn't make sense."

"Eileen, you've got to play this part up more. You're not saying it with meaning!"

And I would start crying and screaming, "I will not mean what I'm saying until air. I've got so many other things to think about. I've got to get the technicalities out of the way so I can play it as it should be played. So I can be real!"

And poor June Gossit, our makeup lady, would have to start making up my eyes all over again, because I would cry off all the mascara and Ted would keep worrying me with his notes. All I can say now is, "God bless all producers and directors for their patience with young actors." When you're new and young and you don't know your way around, it's frightening and frustrating. The pressure of doing a soap is enormous. Fear is a great catalyst for acting irrationally or being difficult. It took me a few months to learn how to talk to Ted and control myself. I began to realize that the producers, writers, and directors were as nervous about hiring me as I was about being hired.

I worked nonstop during the next several months. Every morning I was scheduled to be at Warner Brothers, a long, sleek limousine would pick me up. I would come flying out the door dressed in jeans and sneakers. My doorman must have thought I either had a very rich boyfriend or had changed professions. One day the limo picked me up at the CBS studio to shoot an outdoor evening scene for the movie. I was all dolled up in my swinging hooker outfit. The scene was to take place on the street and all the lights were on. It looked like a block party with people stacked up along the curb to watch the filming.

I was in my trailer waiting for my call when the stage manager came up to me and said, "Eileen, do you know a Bill?"

"I don't know," I replied. I didn't think it was *my* Bill because he was in California.

"Well, he's standing out there and he says you're his ex-wife." The stage manager laughed. "You couldn't have been married. You're too young."

I decided to take a peek and sure enough, there was Bill, leaning against a tree, his trusty umbrella in one hand. I quickly decided I owed him the courtesy of saying hello.

"Maggie, I knew you would make it. I always knew when we were married you would make it and I wouldn't . . ."

"Bill," I fumbled. I didn't know what to say. It was an embarrassing moment—especially with an entire crowd watching our every move, listening to our conversation. "How are you," was about all I could manage.

After exchanging some small talk I told him I had to go. The meeting shook me up because our divorce wasn't final and from the way he looked at me, it appeared he was still interested in pursuing a relationship. A few nights later, I was having a bad time sleeping. I felt tense, worried, anxious. I walked over to the window and pulled up the shade to look at the moon. Imagine my surprise when I saw Bill standing on the street below, staring up at my window. It terrified us both and he called me soon after and apologized. He said he had been in the neighborhood and happened to walk past the building and was just looking up, remembering our days together. I didn't know whether to believe him or not, but when it happened a second time, I decided to find a new apartment. It was the first time in my life anyone had followed me, but it certainly wouldn't be the last.

I had been on the soap for about two months. Lisa was transforming from a sweet college girl into a conniving vixen. Each time I found the chance to hint at marriage to Bob, I turned it into a life or death situation. Ted Cordey began to notice what I was after. He loved my commitment and drive as an actress and helped me find places where I could put it to use within a scene. Lisa was meant to be a temporary character, but I knew she could add spice to the show over a long period. I took advantage of the slightest opportunities to build her character—fighting for her life the way I fought to get an agent or an audition.

It wasn't long before Irna Phillips began to catch on to what I was trying to do. She liked the idea of this cunning, shrewd Lisa stirring up trouble for the Hugheses. And I think she identified with Lisa's stubbornness. Irna was the original birth mother of soaps. She created many of the first for radio and television (*Guiding Light:* 1937 on radio and 1952 on television). Most of the actors, writers, and directors working in soaps today owe their careers to this former Ohio schoolteacher who altered an entire industry. Irna lived and worked in Chicago. She had a special television line set up so she could watch our dress rehearsals and then provide notes. Though she rarely came to New York, Irna had final say on everything to do with the show.

Lisa's character really took off when Irna began writing her in a more manipulative manner. One of the first scenes in which I got to play this aspect of the character took place when Bob caught mononucleosis. Lisa came to visit, looking a little too sexy for a nurse, and she mothered him just the way Nancy, his real mother, would, trying to maneuver her way into the family.

The original Lisa dreamed of marrying the man she loved, living in a sweet little house filled with children, and tending a garden filled with flowers. The Lisa I was playing wanted to marry Bob because he was going to be a doctor, which meant an expensive home, her own car, money, and position. Based on what was happening with the story line, Irna decided to age Bob quickly: The conniving Lisa would secretly marry sweet Bob and then get pregnant. Irna also wanted Bob out of medical school. She loved characters who were doctors and lawyers because she was always in and out of hospitals with all sorts of little ailments. She would get terrific scoops and story ideas while she was convalescing.

Aging Bob was not as easy as it might seem. Ronnie Welch, who played Bob, had an undeniably youthful face. He grew a beard and a mustache, tried smoking, and even wore glasses, but nothing worked. Everyone finally agreed that Ronnie would have to be replaced. Irna liked Don Hastings very much. He had a good reputation and was currently on *The Edge of Night.* They lost him and we got him! It happened very quickly and without any fanfare. Ronnie left on a Tuesday and Don appeared on Thursday with no explanation. No announcer stating that "The part of Bob Hughes is now being played by . . ." Irna thought ignoring the change was the best way to deal with it. Just before Don's first appearance, one of characters said, "Look, here comes Bob. Yes, that's Bob and he's coming this way." Don appeared and that was it.

Nine months later, when Lisa gave birth to her first son, Tom, Ronnie Welch sent a telegram to the studio which read, "Congratulations on the birth of Tom! Funny but he doesn't look like Don. He looks a lot like me!"

One month before my movie, *Girl of the Night,* was to premiere at the Criterion Theater, I got a call to audition for a television commercial. It was for a popular beverage which shall remain nameless (I'm not giving them a free plug!). In the commercial I had to say something to my TV mother about inviting people over for dinner. Then I was supposed to open the refrigerator, grab a bottle of the soft drink, and take a sip. When we shot the first take, the soda spewed and foamed all over me when I popped it open—it hadn't been refrigerated. The director was furious.

"Cut! Cut! Miss Fulton, for God's sake, girl, don't drink it, just pretend."

"I will not indicate drinking. If I'm supposed to drink—I take a drink. It's not that complicated. If you'd just get a cold bottle we won't have a problem."

The director became even more irritated. "For God's sake, can't you just fake it?"

"How am I going to fake drinking if I hold it up and start swallowing?"

"We said fake it and that's what we mean."

I was quickly beginning to realize that the wonderful world of television commercials was not exactly what I had bargained for. My television mother in the commercial was annoyed by my attitude. When I got in place for another take, she snapped, "Do you suppose the little actress can do it this time?" I wanted to take the beverage and pour it on her head.

We began filming another take and it squirted all over my face again, so they had to redo my makeup. After another heated discussion, the director agreed that I could *really* drink and that the bottle should be cold. The next two takes went smoothly and we proceeded to film the next part of the commercial.

Five seconds into the shot the director started screaming again.

"Cut! Cut! Miss Fulton, don't play her like that. You're playing her like a teenager. Make her older."

The four men from the advertising agency were all playing director. Now I had five men telling me what to do. Each had his own idea of who I was supposed to be. After their suggestions, I made her older, younger, like Katharine Hepburn, like me, like Lisa, from the North, from the West, and from the East, until finally one of them cried, "My God, girl, you can't even talk! You don't even have an accent. If we could only identify you with some part of the country, maybe you would be believable." I wondered why they had hired me in the first place.

Suddenly they put all the lights on me. I felt like an insect being studied through a microscope. A voice bellowed over the loudspeaker, "Eileen Fulton, listen to this tape!"

I did. It was the sound track from the first take, when I gagged on the soda because it was so warm. "That's terrible!" the speaker voice announced. Everybody was standing around—the crew and the extras—waiting for the next scene and staring at me as if I were the worst actress in the history of the world.

Finally I had had enough. "You don't know what the hell you want!" *Hell* was a very strong word for me to use—especially in public—at that time. It shocked them so much no one spoke for thirty seconds. "We've got a problem here," I declared. "You want it like this and you want it like that, but the sad truth is you don't know what the hell you really want!"

The voice from the speaker began blaring again. "Quiet her down, take her out, take her to dinner, get her out of here."

The four men from the advertising agency took me to dinner. I was so angry I ordered everything I could think of. One of the men leaned over and said, "You know, we're going to have to let you go. Where did you learn to act?"

"Well," I said, revving my southern engines, "if you want to watch, I'm on *As the World Turns* every day. I've also got a movie opening in a week, and I happen to have the lead. I'll send you a pass. I've never seen such a group of idiots in my life. Nobody knows what he wants and you blame it all on me."

I walked out of the restaurant—and the commercial. I decided that I didn't need to be a star of those sixty-second spots: Theater, soaps, and movies would be more than enough for me!

One day John Conboy, our stage manager, and future producer of *The Young and the Restless,* pulled me aside and said, "Eileen, you need to buy some clothes."

"But I've got two dresses," I replied.

He couldn't believe that I thought two dresses would see me through my career. I had rebelled against so much of who I had been during my adolescent years that I had forgotten that I really enjoyed beautiful clothes and playing dress-up. With John's advice firmly fixed in my mind, I headed for the nearest department store, bought four dresses, shoes and bags to match, and went home and threw up. Spending money on clothes—or anything else—scared me to death. It was a fear I soon overcame. In fact, it wouldn't be long before looking glamorous would become an important part of both Lisa Miller's *and* Eileen Fulton's lives.

My newfound popularity on television enabled me to audition for more plays and musicals. When I began performing the role of Luisa in 1961 in the off-Broadway production of *The Fantasticks,* it was then beginning its second year. Thirty-five years later it's still going as strong as ever—kind of like that Energizer rabbit in the television commercial. By day I was the scheming, conniving Lisa. By night I played a zany, cute kid. I had to give up any sort of social life, however, once I started performances in *The Fantasticks.* My day began at CBS at 7:30 A.M. and ended every night at 11:15 P.M., when I walked out the stage door. It was hard work, but I loved every minute of it. I really had the best of both worlds, working in television by day, earning a very good living, and feeding myself on the laughter and applause of a live audience by night.

I left *The Fantasticks* after eight months and began rehearsals a few weeks later for a production of *Abe Lincoln in Illinois,* starring Hal Holbrook. I was hired to play Annie Rutledge, a spunky tavern maid who teaches Abe to read and eventually becomes his sweetheart. Hal was absolutely adorable. He used to relax backstage by resting his feet on the dressing room table, a big cigar in one hand and a glass of brandy in another.

While I was still performing in *Lincoln,* I got the part of Honey for the matinee company of *Who's Afraid of Virginia Woolf?,* which was being directed by Alan Schneider. Because the play was so grueling to perform, they had a separate cast that performed during the matinees. I signed the contract without telling the producer of *World.* I knew there would be trouble, but felt I could make my case when the time came.

What I hadn't counted on, however, was the time the matinee began. The play, being longer than most, started at 2 P.M. instead of the usual 2:30 P.M. But *World* didn't finish until 2 P.M. How could I be in two places at once? I was frantic.

Helen Wagner, who played my TV mother-in-law, Nancy, solved the problem.

"Now Eileen, before you do anything rash, let's figure this out. I think I know a way to make this work."

At that time, our studio was in Grand Central Station. Helen told me there was a shuttle train that would take me right to the theater if I got on the front car and went out the Forty-first Street exit, right next door to the Billy Rose Theater. She borrowed a stop watch and one day at 2:00 P.M., when we finished the show, she pressed the button and yelled, "Go!" We raced for the elevator, ran to the shuttle train, got on the front car, jumped off at Times Square, dashed up the Forty-first Street exit steps, ran all the way to the theater, shooting past the backstage doorman who must have thought we were a couple of nuts, ran all the way to the stage, and looked at the watch. We made it in ten minutes. It wouldn't take long to get into costume, and I didn't hit the stage until ten minutes after the show began. I was convinced I could do it.

Now all I had to do was convince my new television produ-

cer. I called Bill McCaffrey because he handled my *World* contract and told him of my predicament.

"Don't worry, little girl," he said. "I'll make an appointment for us and between the two of us we can assure him the
play will not pose a conflict."

On the day of the meeting, both Mr. McCaffrey and I made
our case, but the producer was in a particularly unreasonable
mood. "We won't let you do it," he stated matter-of-factly.

I rose to the bait. "I *am* going to do it!!" I declared, "with or
with*out* your permission!!!"

He took my hand into his small sweaty palm, patted it, and
gave me one of those phony condescending smiles. "My dear,
dear Eileen, that will be a breach of contract. We don't want a
breach of contract now, do we?"

I paused for a moment and then drew a long, deep breath, as
if I had suddenly grown tired of the whole thing. And then I
looked him dead in the eye and stated, "We don't have a signed
contract." My renewal contract was on my desk. It had been
sitting there for weeks waiting for my signature. I just hadn't
gotten around to it.

"What do you mean?" he gasped.

"We don't have a signed contract. My old contract is up as
of today, and the new one hasn't been signed."

He turned absolutely white, shot to his desk, pulled out a
file, and sank back into his chair. "My God, you're right. But
you have to sign your contract. You have to renew. You can't
quit the show now!"

"Oh my dear, dear man," I began, trying to mimic the condescending tone he had used on me, "I will be happy to renew,
but you must put in writing that I can do my Broadway show."
Game. Set. Match! McCaffrey sat back in amazement, quite
proud of his client.

The following day I signed my new *World* contract. Three

weeks later I began the matinee performances of *Woolf*.

One afternoon we had a small bonfire on stage. Elaine Stritch, who was playing Martha, accidentally dropped her cigarette ashes down into the couch. Not realizing what she had done, she finished the scene and walked off stage, leaving the two male actors also unaware of what was taking place. In a matter of minutes, smoke started rising from the couch. The audience must have thought it was part of the script. While I was preparing for my next scene, the stage manager ran into my dressing room.

"I hate to interrupt you, Eileen, but we've got a serious problem. The right end of the couch is on fire. Would you please try to put it out when you go on?"

Honey was supposed to be crazy and drunk in her next scene, so I started ad-libbing like mad. "I smell smoke. Oh, everything is going wrong. Even the sofa is burning." I fell back on the couch and poured my bottle of liquor into the side on fire, putting it out. Suddenly the audience realized what was actually going on and started applauding. The next day, the papers wrote about the incident. One article stated, "Eileen Fulton ad-libbed lines Edward Albee never wrote while dousing the blaze with her drinks and her tears."

I stayed with *Woolf* for almost a year, and, just to prove to the world what a workaholic I could be, I also went back to *The Fantasticks* at the same time. I was then doing *World* four to five days a week and *The Fantasticks* every night. Saturdays were rough because I did the *Woolf* matinee, which I also did on Wednesdays, and then two shows back-to-back with *Fantasticks* on Saturday night and two shows on Sunday. Monday was my only day of rest—unless I had to appear on *World*, which was usually the case.

It was a crazy, mixed-up, jam-packed schedule, but I loved every minute of it! Happiness is a great driving force. During my "spare" time I also began to work on a nightclub act. Henry Fanelli, the harpist in *Fantasticks,* and I spent an hour or so after the show working on material. Jan Wallman, who had a show-case club called the Upstairs at the Duplex, let me try out the act on a Sunday night. I fell in love with performing all over again that night. Jan offered me a booking, but the week I was to open the club closed.

After a few months I was beginning to feel overworked and emotionally strung out. I caught a cold. I had been giving serious thought to leaving *World* because Lisa, at that time, had outwitted herself. I felt she had done all the scheming and conniving possible and was rapidly turning into a self-pitying, whining creature. I was getting sick of her and wanted to devote more time to my singing endeavors, as well as have the days to audition for plays and musicals. I explained how I felt to the producer and asked to be released from my contract. We worked out an arrangement where, if I agreed to stay on for three months, I would be released. Irna Phillips made one of her rare appearances in the studio a few days later and asked me why I was leaving.

"Because I feel there are other things I should be doing—or at least trying to do. I want desperately to sing. I feel I've got to try."

Instead of being angry as I expected, Irna smiled and said, "I understand. We must be honest with ourselves." And then she kissed me on the cheek.

Two weeks before I left *World* I quit *Fantasticks.* I wanted to be free to accept something totally new. *Woolf* was on a limited run and would soon close. I tried to imagine what it would be like—for the first time in such a long time—to wake up and not rush out the door.

My last day on the show was a sad one. Helen Wagner came

to my dressing room and we hugged and kissed and cried. Don McLaughlin spoke for the cast and said, "We offer you our love and understanding and best wishes. Please keep in touch because we will always be interested in what you are doing." I think Don admired me at the time for having the courage to leave a sure thing with nothing waiting in the wings. I didn't have an agent, manager, husband, boyfriend, or a job. But I was convinced I was doing the right thing.

I remember walking out of the building and looking up at the late afternoon sun thinking, *I'm free, I'm free.* As I began to walk down the street, however, with no specific sense of direction or purpose, I began to feel lost. It's wildly disorienting when you've been running on a treadmill for over a year and you suddenly push the "stop" button. Who knew when I would find my next job or see my dear, sweet friends from *World* again?

Who, indeed!?

FOUR  ~

# Even the Corpse Won't Come

*A*s soon as *Woolf* closed in 1963, I finally allowed my body to collapse. Of course I immediately got sick and was diagnosed with a mild case of walking pneumonia.

"You have two choices," my doctor said with an authoritative gleam in her eye. "You can either check yourself into the hospital or take a two-week holiday in the Virgin Islands."

That was all it took to convince me: Twenty-four hours later I was at the airport, waiting to board a plane headed for St. Thomas. Being nervous about the trip, I wanted to get to the airport early. Two of my friends drove me. We had a drink to toast a pleasant trip and then they left. It was eight o'clock but my plane wasn't due to leave until eleven. I decided to have dinner, including a glass of wine and an after-dinner drink with my coffee. I then walked around the airport until ten thirty, headed toward the gate, and promptly took a Dramamine so I wouldn't get airsick. Five minutes later the alcohol and pills kicked in. I was ready to collapse and sleep for a week. I was afraid to sit down for fear I'd zonk out and miss the plane. Imagine my disappointment when the flight was delayed until 3 A.M. and I had to keep myself awake.

While I was waiting, a woman dressed completely in white approached me.

"Do you speak English?"

I nodded, wondering who she was and what she wanted. Outfitted in white pants, white jacket, and a white fur, she made quite an impression. A very mousey-looking young woman stood beside her. They appeared to be traveling together.

"We're flying on your plane and I thought we could sit together and chat to pass the time."

All I wanted to do was sleep. By now, after all those hours of standing, I was ready to drop, but I didn't want to hurt her feelings. It was a three-seats-across plane, so there I was, stuck in the middle. The lady in white was so overly friendly I began to wonder if she was some new breed of pickpocket. Perhaps I was getting paranoid from the pills and wine, but I was afraid that if I went to sleep she might steal all my money and traveler's checks.

My "new best friend" began telling me her life story. She was a high-class call girl who ran an abortion ring in Puerto Rico. She told me she wore only white and drove a white Lincoln Continental. She was taking the young girl to Puerto Rico for an abortion. Miss Winter Wonderland then gave me her card and assured me that if I ever needed a "job" she would take good care of me.

I wasn't certain if she meant a job as a prostitute or a job as an abortionist, but either way I wasn't interested in filling out an application. I was terrified of that card because if the plane crashed and it was found in my possession, what would my parents think? I could just imagine the headlines. I tore it up into little pieces and threw it away in the airplane's lavatory just to be safe. I didn't feel completely safe until we landed and said good-bye to each other.

I spent most of my two weeks in St. Thomas alone, sleeping. I did meet a lovely couple in the dining room one evening. Just before I was to return, I decided to go to town to shop. The husband saw me in the lobby and asked where I was going.

"I'm grabbing a cab into town to find out if that duty-free shopping is as great as everyone says it is."

"If you visit a perfume shop would you buy a bottle of Joy for me?" he asked. "It's a gift for my secretary, but please don't tell my wife."

I felt like a conspirator, but agreed to help him for the sake of keeping up office relations.

Just as I was getting in a cab, his wife saw me and asked if I wanted to share a ride into town with her. I agreed and we ended up shopping together. I bought a few bottles of perfume for myself and the Joy for my companion's husband, hoping she couldn't read my mind. I saw her at the other counter buying several bottles of men's cologne.

She giggled and said, "Promise you won't tell my husband. I'm not shopping with him in mind."

I assumed they had an "understanding" and decided the poor husband deserved to have one "friend," since his wife was obviously shopping for several.

By the end of my two-week stay, I was ready to return to New York.

*World* hired a new Lisa as soon as I left. They picked a girl whose voice and appearance were similar to my own. During her first two weeks, they shot her only from the back so the audience still thought I was playing the role.

When actors leave soaps, the writers' imaginations go into overdrive trying to find a "reasonable" way to handle the transition. *World*'s writers were no exception. Lisa was supposed to be suffering from shock and could not bear to look at anyone. She had apparently been kidnaped by three men who raped her repeatedly from California to Texas in the back of a black limousine; consequently, she lost her mind. Of course, Lisa had to narrate what had happened to her—you couldn't begin to show such provocative scenes on daytime—not then at least!

After about two weeks of keeping her face from the audience, the writers had one of the characters finally say, "Lisa, take down your hands and look at me." There was a dramatic pause while the new actress slowly uncovered her face. At that instant all of the action on the screen froze and the voice of Dan McCullough (the announcer) said, "The part of Lisa Hughes is now being played by. . . ." Soap announcers always have those big, booming, authoritative voices—kind of like how you'd imagine God sounded when he gave Moses those Ten Commandments. It was not a voice to be questioned.

The new Lisa gave it her best shot, but she had walked into the difficult situation of replacing an actress with whom the audience had developed such a definite love-hate relationship. Phone calls started coming through by the hundreds and letters and telegrams by the thousands, begging for the return of the *real* Lisa. Even the newspapers picked up on it, printing silly items like "Where is the real Lisa? She must be an alcoholic in hiding after playing Honey for so long."

I was obviously flattered and quickly learned that no matter what kind of publicity you get, it's beneficial to your career. Most soap viewers don't realize how much power they have: Enough letters, telegrams, and phone calls can kill characters and story lines or turn a temporary part (like Lisa) into a long-term love affair.

A few months later, I was at Ruth Bailey's Cherry County Playhouse in Michigan performing in a stock production of *Grand Prize*. Irna Phillips telephoned one day to dangle a tantalizing piece of bait.

"We're thinking of using some of the characters from *World* to develop a nighttime series. I don't see why you shouldn't be a part of it. And I've got a marvelous new story line for Lisa." She went on to explain that since *Peyton Place* was doing so well,

CBS had decided they should have a nighttime series, too. They realized in my absence how important Lisa had become to the viewers—the real Lisa—so Irna hinted that if the show materialized, the role would be mine. Lisa was to begin a new life for herself in Chicago and bring in, from time to time, the *World* characters. In turn, she would also make occasional appearances on *World*. The network hoped to get the daytime viewers to watch the nighttime series.

I was definitely tempted. Even at that young age, I felt that no one would ever write for me as well as Irna did. She allowed an actor to build a character and then wrote scenes inspired by those nuances the actor brought to the part. The possibility of a nighttime series—how could I refuse?

Two months after I returned to *World,* I signed on to do the nighttime series. The original title of the show was *The Woman Lisa,* but it was eventually changed to *Our Private World.* The series was the first nighttime soap for CBS. Since the network wanted to make a big impression, we had a huge budget for sets and costumes. To help publicize the show, someone at CBS came up with a terrific idea that revolved around Grandpa's (played by Santos Ortega) birthday on *World*. Grandpa was a real down home character and the viewers loved him.

Each day for almost two weeks, our announcer asked the viewers to help wish Grandpa a happy birthday by sending him a card. I think we got seventeen million cards! The publicity department used the responses to create a mailing list for *Our Private World*. They wrote a letter to the show's fans which read, "Dear Friends, I am leaving my home and family behind in Oakdale. Please wish me well and watch me as I continue my life every Wednesday and Friday night in *Our Private World.* Love, Lisa." To this day, fans still show up with the letter when I do personal appearances and ask me to sign it.

I received a tremendous amount of publicity at the time. But when I read one columnist describe me as a "frumpy little thing," I made up my mind then and there to become more glamorous—I just wasn't quite sure how. I started asking everybody for ideas and tips. Rosemary Prinz, who played Penny on *World,* suggested a cosmetician she thought was very good. For forty bucks I would be taught how to properly apply makeup in two hours. It seemed like a lot of money, but I decided that experimenting with different products would undoubtedly cost more, so I made the appointment. It was worth the expense a thousand times over. I still had to worry about my clothes, though. That problem wouldn't be resolved for a few more months.

Lisa made her last appearance on *World* on May 3, 1965. She was on a train going to Chicago and as the train pulled out of the station the announcer said, "Follow the adventures of Lisa Hughes beginning tonight on *Our Private World.*" That night, the show opened with me sitting in the club car on the train. I pulled off my wedding ring and dumped it in the ashtray because Bob and I were getting a divorce. My nighttime career was off and running!

Unfortunately, I was pulled out of the race before I had even finished my first lap. Four months later the series was canceled. Irna left right after *Our Private World* opened, and with too many new characters and not enough of Lisa, the show lost its focus— and consequently its viewers. I made it quite clear to the producers that I had no desire to return to *World,* but agreed to come back for an additional ten weeks to give them a chance to wrap up the character. The plan was to have Lisa fall in love with a rich gentleman named John Eldridge who lived in Chicago. She would marry him and settle down to a cozy but luxurious life.

I had a couple of free weeks before the story line was to begin, so I used the time by working on my nightclub act, hiring Sidney Shaw—a musical arranger who worked with Lena

Horne and Leslie Gore—to help me. At the same time, I began studying with a vocal coach named Dori Davis. Dori had been the assistant musical director for *Bye, Bye Birdie* and had taken the show on the road. She was a marvelous teacher who believed in my vocal abilities.

Sidney was concerned about my going on the road alone. He thought Dori would make the perfect escort. She could manage everything and look after me. It wasn't long before I decided to officially make her my manager. One of the first things Dori said when I signed with her was, "If you want to be a star, dress like one."

I began exploring the world of women's dress shops. One day, I walked into Ruth Roman's on Madison Avenue in the hopes of finding an evening dress for my nightclub act. I was attended to by Miss Frankie, a woman of impeccable style and taste. Miss Frankie not only became my personal shopper and fashion consultant, she became one of my best friends. For the past thirty years Miss Frankie has selected all of my clothes—from slacks and suits to fancy evening gowns—both on screen and off.

In a matter of weeks, I returned to *World* to begin the end of Lisa. I had been so involved with my nightclub act, I hadn't given any thought to *World,* but the afternoon I sat in the rehearsal room with the cast, going over the script, it was like attending a funeral. I suddenly understood what was happening to the Lisa I had worked so hard to create. I was the reason she was being written out forever and I felt guilty. The producers learned from the last time when they tried to replace me that it wouldn't work. The viewers would not accept anyone else. In a way, I felt like I was committing murder. I gave Lisa life and now I was acting out a plot that would take her off the air into a permanent retreat where she would remain, unseen by her *World* fans.

As painful as it was playing out Lisa's swan song over the next ten weeks, I believed at the time it was the right thing for me to do. On my last day, I left the studio as quickly as I could because I didn't want to think about it. Life constantly asks us to make choices, giving up one thing for something else. I was giving up Lisa because I couldn't play her and pursue my singing career at the same time. The cast seemed to sense my efforts at containing my emotions. They said little other than to wish me luck and asked that I keep in touch with them.

I began touring my nightclub act across the country, performing in supper clubs and hotels from Ohio to Texas. When I got to Beaumont, I found out that hundreds of people had checked into the hotel where I was singing just to see me. The manager said I was the first television personality to bring him that kind of business. I was tremendously grateful that my fans were so supportive. After one of my shows a tall, elegantly attired gentleman approached me and said I had ruined his business.

"Lisa, you are my worst enemy. I'm a funeral director, I can't schedule funerals between one thirty and two o'clock when your show is on the air. No one would show up—not even the corpse!"

It wasn't long before CBS was once again flooded with phone calls, telegrams, and letters demanding the return of Lisa. I was very flattered, naturally, but was not going to do anything unless I felt strongly compelled. CBS started tracking me down, making irresistible offers. I missed the show and the character, but I couldn't even consider the idea until I completed the nightclub tour. The more I worked the clubs, however, the more I realized it was Lisa they wanted. One night, just as I walked on the stage, I heard a woman whisper to her husband, "See? There she is. There's that awful Lisa now. You thought she was living in Chicago, married to that rich John Eldridge.

She obviously left her husband and son just so she could sing in nightclubs. That's the kind of hussy woman she is!"

That was the type of fan I attracted. Individuals who were so absorbed in the character they could never separate Eileen Fulton from Lisa Miller Hughes Eldridge.

When I returned to New York, I had made up my mind to go back to *World*. I learned a great deal during my nightclub tour: Lisa had a following that would be foolish to ignore. Those who hated her apparently needed to have someone on whom they could vent. Those who loved her no doubt enjoyed her adventures vicariously. I learned, most of all, that I could sing and hold an audience no matter how difficult the conditions. If *World* would give me time off to do theater, movies, and club acts *and* let me return as a glamorous, sophisticated woman, I would go back. I thought the new image would work well with the new story line. If Lisa had really gone off to Chicago to marry the rich John Eldridge, she certainly would come back to Oakdale flaunting her latest and most expensive acquisitions.

Everyone on the show just about dropped their jaw when I arrived that first day back in 1966. I swept in wearing a gorgeous mink and a contemporary new hair style. I had come a long way, thanks to Miss Frankie, from the sweet little girl who had only two dresses with hanger marks on the shoulders. As I entered the rehearsal hall, some of the cast jumped up and rushed over to hug me. Everybody was chattering at once. It was like being welcomed back into a family. I don't know if they knew how much I missed them, but I surely did. When I walk into that studio every day, it's like walking into another life with my *other* family.

Cort Steen, who was directing that day and was known for his large frame, almost crushed me with his enthusiasm.

"I had forgotten how little you are," he said as he took my face in his hands.

Helen Wagner looked so beautiful. She was wearing a magnificent lynx hat and a beige lace dress that perfectly matched the color of the hat. Seeing her again warmed me all over. She's such a down-to-earth, unaffected lady. And a fantastic cook to boot!

I remember one time, just after joining *World,* I overheard Helen giving somebody a recipe for a stew that sounded so good I found myself drooling. I had never heard of peppercorns then, but in those days of grits and more grits, I hadn't heard of a lot of things. The first time I ever saw chives in a grocery store I thought it was grass. What did I know back then? I thought New Yorkers were so cute buying little pots of grass to put a feeling of the country in their apartments.

Helen's stew recipe was my first attempt to do "fancy" cooking and it opened up a whole new and wonderful world for me. I started buying cookbooks and began to explore recipes and started growing my own fresh herbs. I now pride myself on being quite a cook. Over the years I've collected some fantastic recipes from my fans—one day it might make a fun cookbook. But it was because of Helen's interest in food that I really became excited about cooking.

Knowing the people you work with is the key to giving a good show day after day. You have something to identify with immediately when playing a scene. Helen liked to garden, so when I first joined the show I knew something about her as a human being, something I could relate to, which made it easier to have a natural response to the character.

There were two individuals on the show I had a hard time getting to know. The first was Rosemary Prinz, who played Penny. It might have been a personality conflict, I don't know, but it was completely unnecessary. We didn't realize it until it was too late, but all during the early years we never bothered to take the time to get to know each other. Our scenes were always antagonistic, but I hate to think that the story line influenced the effort we made to develop a friendship.

It wasn't until I returned to *World* in 1966 that we became good friends. That came about because we discovered we had something in common—a passion for singing. Rosemary had done a lot of nightclub work, so we began to compare notes about club acts and repertoire. Unfortunately, shortly after I came back, Rosemary left. She had been with *World* for twelve years, since the beginning in 1956.

There was a farewell party for Rosemary at a fancy east side restaurant. After a lovely dinner, as we were walking to the door, she suddenly ran up to me. We threw our arms around each other and cried, because we had wasted almost ten years of not knowing each other just because we hadn't taken the time.

The other individual I had a personality conflict with was Roy Schuman. He played Michael Shea, the wicked doctor. From our first scene together I didn't like him. He was charming, but there was just something about the chemistry that put me off. It was a difficult situation because I, as Lisa, had decided he was going to be my new lover. I had to really work at making it convincing. You can't just say your lines. You've got to find something about a person to love if you're supposed to play a love scene. I found myself arguing with him and fighting when we weren't on the set. It was an impossible situation, and I didn't have a rational explanation for my reaction.

Our story line together was getting hot and heavy, and I thought, *I've got to find something to love about him because I'm going to kiss him and throw myself at him and wear all these sexy negligees and seduce him. I've got to find something . . .*

One day Roy said, "Eileen, my mother is in town visiting me and I would like to do something very special for her. I've always admired the hats you wear, and I wondered if you could recommend a hat shop?"

I was flattered that he would ask me and thought it was so sweet of him to want to buy something lovely for his mother. After that when I played a scene with him, I looked at Roy in an entirely different light. I used the idea that he cared about his mother, which gave me something to love about him. In time, I began to analyze why I hadn't liked him. Suddenly I realized he looked just like that awful boy, Jimmy, back in high school, who threw my books out of his locker and called me a slut. Once I knew what the problem was, we got along fine and became good friends, until he was murdered—on the show, that is.

The first scene for my big return in 1966 took place in the Chicago house with my son Tom—played by the marvelous actor Richard Thomas, best known for his role as John Boy on *The Waltons*. Tom was helping me pack my bags, excited at the prospect of escorting his mother back to Oakdale. The new me with the blond hair hardly resembled the mousy, brown-haired girl they last saw. While I was packing, they did a flashback of the scene that had taken place two years earlier in the hospital. I was pleading with Bob to marry me again and our baby was sick. Bob shoved me away saying he didn't love me anymore. He calmly walked away and I collapsed crying hysterically on the floor until he was out of sight. Then I let loose with a mad insane laugh so uncontrollable it frightened me as well as the cast. It was a very dramatic, very "Lisa" kind of scene.

About a week later, I received a letter from a fan. "Welcome back, Lisa dear. I'm so happy you decided to come back, but don't you see what they did to you back then? You look so pretty now and so healthy. Please don't let them do that to you again."

Up until that year, I had never had an appetite; I could go days without eating if I didn't keep a constant watch over my neglectfulness. I don't know what Freud would say, but when I returned I was constantly hungry. One day I had a dinner scene to do with my TV mother, Ethel Remy. She was supposed to say, "Lisa, stop picking at your food. Eat, dear." And I wasn't supposed to eat because we had had an argument and I was very upset.

That morning during the first rehearsal, I took one look at those lamb chops, the mashed potatoes, green beans, tossed salad, and rolls and my mouth fell apart wider than the Grand Canyon itself! Our prop department had certainly come a long way from that first day in the Sweet Shop when I drank sour milk shakes topped with a few squirts of shaving cream. Since it was only a rehearsal, I ate the whole plate. At 11 A.M. we rehearsed the scene again. Again, I couldn't resist so I ate another plate of food. At 12:30 P.M. we had a dress rehearsal and, once again, I came, I saw, I digested everything in sight! Everybody in the control room was hysterical by now.

Just before we went live, the director winked and asked me if I would please be careful not to eat until *after* Ethel had asked me to—and then to only take *one* bite. I promised. As soon as the scene was over, however, Ethel joined me. Together we had another wonderful meal. Herbie, our prop man then, cooked all the meals himself and was quite a chef. Of course, when I weighed myself a few days later, I discovered I had gained nine pounds!

Most actors don't like to eat and talk with a mouth full of food, but I love it. It's real life. One time we had a fancy dinner scene with Chris, Grandpa, Dick Martin, and myself. I was supposed to serve cherries jubilee. We had very few lines in which to eat the dish, after which I was supposed to say, "Let's go out to the garden."

Well, all morning I tried to get the dessert to catch fire, but it wouldn't ignite. We kept pouring more and more brandy into the dish. By air time we had completely drenched the dessert.

When I next lit it on the air, it burst into flames like a rocket taking off.

When you do live television you learn one important rule: No matter what happens, you keep playing through the scene. I spooned the red hot cherries onto the ice cream, trying to blow the flames out. I looked across at Chris and he was actually eating the flaming cherries! "Oh, now, Chris, be careful," I began ad-libbing. "Watch out for those flames."

I could hear the glass dishes starting to crack and prayed the scene would end before we all went up in smoke. Grandpa started pouring ice cream over the mess in front of him, trying to put an end to the crisis.

"Grandpa," I laughed, "go on now, put out your fire!" That was the only time I can ever remember that real liquor was used for a show. And it was the only time I saw the entire cast "looped." We had been eating cherries soaked in brandy all morning until air.

I quickly learned to overcome whatever "technical" difficulties we experienced in live television. Every line and every action is timed to the second. It was drilled into us at every opportunity, "No matter what happens, keep going, keep going!" Having been trained in the theater, I already knew that "the show must go on"—*even if it means risking death!*

One day I was taping one of those wonderful hospital scenes. Lisa was supposed to be dying of pneumonia, so I was encased in an oxygen tent. After the dress rehearsal, the director decided to get a new tent because the one they had been using was so old and wrinkled you couldn't see my face. The new tent arrived within minutes of air time. During the dress rehearsal, they had unzipped the tent in the back so I could breathe, but in the rush to get us in place, they forgot to unzip the new tent. There I was locked in an airtight plastic bag on live television. I had no lines, naturally, since I was near death. I was supposed to just lie there and gasp as the camera started tightening in on me.

After about fifteen minutes I realized I couldn't breathe. I began to tingle all over. Suddenly Herbie saw my problem. He tried to crawl around behind the bed to unzip the tent, but the camera would have caught him, so there was nothing he could do. The instant the shot was over, Herbie threw back the plastic and slapped me in the face because I was out of it.

I don't think I've ever been so frightened, but I couldn't stop the show. My lips, hands, and nails were blue. Our show was in color. Everybody who watched that day wrote in commenting on how realistic the dying Lisa looked. I'm willing to do a lot of things to make a role more convincing, but *dying* isn't one of them!

Fast costume changes proved to be one of the most challenging aspects of performing a live show. One particular day I had to do three complete changes and restyle my hair (we had to do our hair back then—no fancy professionals who would fluff you and frost you into a magnificently coifed creature). And we were working in a new studio space at the time, so I wasn't very familiar with the placement of all the sets. Television soap studios are like big basketball courts that have been subdivided into little playing areas containing all of the necessary locations for that particular show. It's like a big maze of furniture and walls— and it's very easy to get lost.

On this particular day, I had to play a flirting scene with Bruce. The second it ended, they cut to black for the commercial break. A voice from the darkness announced, "You have thirty-two seconds." I literally had to run to the other end of the studio where the next scene was going to take place. The wardrobe assistant began ripping my clothes off and zipping me up in a new dress. I prayed that the zipper wouldn't break. Sometimes they came apart and you just had to keep your back away from the camera and try to sit and stand and appear natural even though it looked like you had some form of paralysis.

My zipper held that day—thank God!—and I began my scene with baby Tom. I sang him a song and then walked into his nursery, which was off camera, to put him to bed. When I returned to the living room, Tom was supposed to cry. The show had hired a woman named Madeline who made her living going from soap to soap crying like a baby. She was quite remarkable and took her job very seriously. When she arrived for rehearsal, she would ask, "Is this supposed to be a tired cry? A sick cry? An 'I miss my mommy' cry?" I asked her one day how she got her job. She told me she had a roommate several years before who was also an actress. Whenever the roommate wanted to get rid of a date, she would say, "Excuse me, I have to check in on my baby now" and then Madeline would start her imitation.

As soon as my scene with the baby ended, I had to run back to the other end of the studio to do another scene with Bruce. Of course I had to change into a short evening dress, apply evening makeup, and restyle my hair—all in forty-five seconds! I was in a panic all day over the changes, worrying that I would run to the wrong set or trip on a cable. I later found out that Ted Cordey got the biggest kick out of watching me running around the maze of the studio floor like a mouse in a scientific experiment trying to find the cheese.

Sometimes we'd be near the end of the scene and our stage manager, John Conboy, would start signaling with his hands to either speed up or slow down. He always tried to be discreet, but I could see it in my peripheral vision and it drove me mad. I would lose concentration realizing that I was on live television in front of 23 million viewers.

The first and last time John ever gave me a "speed up," a signal to pick up the pace, I froze in the middle of a fight with Don Hastings. I stared at him panic-stricken and said, "Bob, it's up to you." Don, the consummate professional, summed up my speech and we finished the scene. After that, John was always careful to stay out of my sightline when he had to give anyone a signal.

Taping a live soap on a daily basis is a tense and strenuous occupation—not unlike walking through a minefield. You try to reach the end of a scene and hope that nothing unexpectedly explodes along the way. Many years ago I endured one particular "explosion" that has made it difficult for me to drink coffee ever since.

During one very popular story line, the wicked doctor Michael Shea was trying to get back at Lisa by proving she was an unfit mother. In one of his attempts to frame Lisa, he made certain their son got hold of some sleeping pills—not enough to kill him, but enough to scare Lisa. Michael made it look like it was Lisa's fault. Lisa finds her son with the sleeping pills, becomes hysterical, and can't believe her carelessness. As a public service, the producers decided to write into the scene what should be done if a similar incident occurred in anyone's home. Soaps have always tried to educate their viewers, whenever possible.

I didn't know it at the time, but you're supposed to give the overdosed individual a coffee enema until the doctor arrives. The producers asked the mother of the little boy who was playing my son Chuck if the doctor could pull down the child's pajama bottom to make it look more realistic when he was giving the shot. The mother and child agreed. During the live dress rehearsal, which is carried to all of the affiliates across the country, the doctor began to pull down the boy's pajamas to give him the shot. The child must have suddenly realized that his bare bottom was about to be exposed for all the world to see. He began to squirm and whimper. The doctor, trying to calm the boy, ad-libbed by saying, "Oh, it's nothing. It's just a little prick!"

We all thought we'd just about die with laughter. Ethel, who played my mother, was holding the enema bag. She was noted for never breaking up no matter what happened. In an attempt to control her laughter, Ethel clutched the bag so hard it exploded. Coffee splattered all over the room. We couldn't get through the rest of the live dress.

After a lunch break, we began the live show and everything went perfectly: The child didn't squirm; the doctor didn't ad-lib; no one laughed. The next scene, for which we had only sixty seconds to get into place, was in the kitchen. We're all sitting around the table, comforting each other, relieved that we overcame a potential tragedy. What we forgot, however, was that we're all supposed to be drinking *coffee!* Each of us stared at the thick, dark liquid in our mugs, and, remembering what had occurred in live dress, we lost all control. We couldn't look at one another. I pretended I was crying with relief from the scene before, but I admit I was really laughing hysterically tears and all.

Because I no longer considered the show a threat to my other creative desires, I could finally relax and enjoy my work. Perhaps that accounted for my increased appetite. I could now appreciate the show more and, I hoped, give it more of myself. During my tour, I learned how important and powerful our show was. Over 20 million people watched every single day back then. That's a lot of viewers. Not only was I happy to be back on *World,* I was proud to be a part of it. Not long after my return, something happened to affirm my new belief in the show.

I had just finished tearing my closets apart one evening when Van Cliburn, the internationally acclaimed pianist, called and said he had just that minute arrived from Texas. I had met Van when I was performing in Neil Simon's *Star Spangled Girl* at the Cherry County Playhouse in Michigan. Interlachen, a nation-ally reknown summer music camp, was located near the Playhouse, and Van was doing a concert and lecturing the students. One of his assistants sent word to the Playhouse that Van was a big fan of mine and wanted to invite me to dinner. I was absolutely thrilled with the idea and said I'd be honored to accept.

Our "date" took place at a beautiful restaurant. When I arrived, I was surprised to realize that the entire place had been reserved for our meeting. Apparently, Van didn't want us to be distracted by fans or autograph seekers. I was impressed that he had gone to so much trouble. The head waiter escorted me to a lovely table with a magnificent arrangement of flowers in the center. After I'd been seated for about five minutes, one of the waiters notified me that Mr. Cliburn's limo had just pulled up and that he would be joining me shortly.

I was so nervous I felt faint. I thought, *Oh, dear God, what am I going to say to this musical genius?* For once in my life I was totally speechless. I heard voices near the entrance to the restaurant and looked up to find this handsome, lanky young man with curly hair. Just as I was about to stand up to say hello, Van screamed from across the room.

"Ahhleen"—he had a thick Texas accent—"my darlin' lovely lady. I've been wanting to meet you for the longest time." He jumped over the tables, used those long legs to sprint across the room, and took me by the hands. "Ahleen, Ahleen, Ahleen, I can't believe it's you!"

We didn't stop talking from the moment he arrived. We chatted about grits, the South, dogs and cats, and compared notes about our lives as children. I felt as if I'd found a long-lost friend.

When I confided that I had wanted to be an opera singer, he announced, "Darlin', we've got to get together and go to an opera." Of course I said I'd love to, but didn't really believe it would happen.

It was almost a year later that he telephoned with a last-minute invitation. He knew it was terrible to ask me out on such short notice, but he hoped I would accept his invitation to hear Renata Tebaldi at the Metropolitan Opera. I have worshiped and adored Tebaldi all of my life. I was already out the door just hearing her name, but reality quickly stuck its foot out and tripped me.

"Van, I just can't," I moaned. "I've got a show to do tomorrow so my alarm is set for five thirty in the morning. I still haven't memorized the scenes. I feel terrible because I'm a big fan but—"

"Now, Ahleen," he interjected, "I certainly can appreciate your commitment to your work schedule, but it's going to be such a wonderful performance and she's a dear friend of mine, so I must go. You told me you loved her. Isn't meeting the great Tebaldi worth losing a little sleep?"

He plead his case better than the most experienced trial attorney. "How much time do I have?"

"Thirty minutes."

I promised to be ready.

I still had on my makeup from the show, so I patched it up, took a five-minute bath, zipped into an evening dress, sprayed perfume all over me, sailed a mink over my shoulders, and flew out the door. All that work doing fast changes on the show was really starting to pay off. Van was waiting for me in a black stretch limo, which sped us away. When we arrived, the doors were already closed. No one is ever seated at the Met once the doors are swung shut, but the ushers recognized Van so they let us in. My peacock feathers were spread full wing as we walked down the aisle. Everybody was staring at us. Even the maestro turned to nod at him. It was very exciting.

Between each act, we had drinks with the great impresario Sol Hurok. He entertained us with marvelous stories. But nothing could compare to Tebaldi. Hearing a magnificent opera singer is one of the most powerful experiences. It's as if the voice itself lifts you from your seat and thrusts you into the middle of the aria, the emotion, the character, the circumstances—until you can't help but feel as though everything is happening to *you*. It doesn't always work, but when it does, nothing compares.

While the bravos were echoing in my ears, we raced backstage. I was more nervous than I'd been in years at the prospect of meeting this dramatic diva. Before Van had a chance to introduce me, Renata extended her expressive arms in my direction, crying, "Lisa, Lisa! You bad, bad girl!"

I nearly fainted from delight. One of my idols, whom I had loved all of my life, knew Lisa. She told me she was a *World* watcher and had been furious that particular day because her set went on the blink just as she was about to settle in for her daily dose.

Lying in bed that night, I could hardly sleep. Renata Tebaldi was a fan of mine!

(LEFT) Smiling for the camera on my first birthday in 1934. (CENTER) When I was two years old, I raced through the neighborhood on my tricycle. (RIGHT) I had this portrait taken for my eighth birthday.

(AT LEFT) Daddy took this picture of Mother and me standing in our backyard on Staten Island.

(AT RIGHT) Wearing my Easter "finest" in Marion.

Playing mother to my brothers, Charles and Jimmy.

These were the first professional photos I had taken. (*Courtesy of Marga Kassimir*)

An early publicity photo of me—and one of my favorites.

Bill and I smile for the camera just seconds before saying "I do."

The newlyweds prepare to embark on their honeymoon.

Bill and I being congratulated by my grandmother and Uncle Tokie.

Me with David Whorf in *One for the Dame,*
which closed before making it to Broadway.
(*Courtesy of Friedman-Abeles*)

*Summer of the Seventeenth Doll* directed by th
great Alan Schneider.
(*Courtesy of Friedman-Abeles*)

Ann Francis and me in
*Girl of the Night.* I loved
working with her.

his was the first "official" photo of Lisa on *TWT*.

Showing off my new shoes to Helen Wagner.

Playing the mealy-mouthed boozer, Honey, in *Who's Afraid of Virginia Wolf* with Billy Berger. (*Courtesy of Billy Berger*)

My return to *The Fantastiks* in 1963. I was doing *Who's Afraid of Virginia Wolf* and *ATWT* at the same time.

The studio released this photo to announce "Lisa's back on *ATWT*" in 1966.

Don Hastings and Dagne Crane camp it up with me during a photo shoot on the set of *ATWT*.

Don Hastings (Bob Hughes) and me with our soap son, Tom, played by Peter Galman.

When I sang for a network publicity event in Chicago I met some of the more interesting members of the CBS family.

A wonderful meeting with my parents at the airport when I flew down to North Carolina to buy them a house. (*Courtesy of Malcolm Gamble*)

One of the few times I visited my mother when she sat down and actually let me serve her.

I've always prided myself on being a woman of 1,000 hats! (*Courtesy of UPI*)

Amelia and I relaxing in our lovely New York apartment.

Preparing for a lovely dinner at home.

# FIVE

# A Smoky Wedding Cake

began to think a lot about the press and how I might be able to use publicity to further my career. It seems like an obvious idea—after all, movie stars and Broadway actors had publicists—but at the time, daytime actors were consciously left out of the network's publicity machine. I become very friendly with the press department at CBS, which was run by a lot of cigar-chomping men who did not take kindly to "little ladies" infiltrating their territory. One of the publicists, Gene Schrott, was the exception to that rule. He helped me on the side.

I kept trying to convince the one female of the department, Dottie Leffler, to work with me. Dottie was in charge of instigating stories in movie magazines and planting items about CBS's nighttime actors to increase their popularity. She didn't want to deal with me or anyone in daytime because, as she said, "the network doesn't feel you're important enough."

"Now Dottie," I began in my best cheerleader tone, "don't you think the fans would love it if in one of those magazines there was a section devoted to the soaps?"

Except for Gene, everyone just laughed at me. Dottie thought the whole idea was silly. "Eileen, who would want to read about some daytime actors anyway?" (This was before publications such as *Soap Opera Digest* existed. Established in 1975, it boasts a current circulation of over one million.)

One of the "good ol' boys" stretched his feet out on the desk, blew cigar smoke into the air, and laughed, saying, "You just stick to daytime, little girl, and worry about your job, and we'll take care of ours."

"No," I insisted. "You don't realize what's going on. This could be big. You really should have a soap opera magazine."

They all thought that was the funniest thing they had heard all week.

Like everything in my life, I decided if no one was going to help me I'd just do it myself. I hired a press agent and started talking about Lisa and the show and my minister's daughter background—it made for great copy, considering what a "bad girl" Lisa was. The producers of *World* were not pleased and told me straight out, "You can't do publicity. You'll ruin the show!"

They were afraid—and I'm convinced they were taking their orders from Irna—that the television viewers would lose interest in our characters or become confused if they saw us as "real" people. Irna always said she wanted the viewing audience to think of us as Bob and Lisa and Nancy—never as Don or Eileen or Helen. I thought it was a lot of nonsense, and was not going to be intimidated or deterred by the producers or Irna. When they said, "NO!" I paused for a moment and just smiled at them. Mustering as much of my southern charm as I could, I calmly replied, "Oh, my dear, sweet, lovely producers. I have already done publicity. I have been doing it since I was a little girl performing in my mama's backyard and my daddy's church. And I will continue to do it wherever I go. So please, *please* don't tell me I can't or I'll just have to leave the show again!" And I meant it!

Bucking tradition, I became the first daytime actor to hire a personal publicist. I believed in it then and I believe in it today.

Considering the fact that we currently live in a world where reality is often shaped by publicists or, as is the case with politicians, professional "spinners," I guess I was just a little bit ahead of my time.

I decided to take advantage of the new provision in my *World* contract that allowed me time off to pursue other interests. After a few months, I went back to the Cherry County Playhouse in Michigan to do *Any Wednesday*. Going back somewhere you've been is a great way to gauge how far you've come. I didn't look anything like the mousy, brown-haired girl who had appeared at the Playhouse a year before, staying at a five-dollar-a-week "Hotel, Hotel, Hotel" (will I ever forget that flashing red neon sign?). I was now a well-dressed blonde with a manager, a beautiful new baby Pekinese, named Amelia Earhart, and a dozen pieces of matching luggage all waiting to be checked into the largest suite at the beautiful Park Place Motor Inn with a glorious view overlooking the lake.

People around those parts remembered that I loved to fish, but the way I looked on this trip, they found it hard to believe I had ever allowed such well-manicured fingernails to brush up against the scales of a freshly caught one. The television news people asked if I would let them film me while I was fishing and I agreed. It rained so hard every day I thought they wouldn't expect me to go sloshing about in weather like that. But I wanted to prove my sportsmanship. They asked if I would pretend to fish just long enough to get some film. Well, ever the professional actress, that's just the sort of faking it I have never liked to do.

I decided that if I camped it up by dressing in a sexy, glamorous outfit, the viewers would know it wasn't like a real day of fishing and I wouldn't feel like I was a phony. When the cameramen arrived they found me decked out in a gorgeous hostess pantsuit and wearing high, jeweled heels. They didn't say anything, but I knew they were wondering what had happened to my faithful faded jeans.

They thought I was going to just pretend to fish but I've always hated just going through the motions. I scraped up a dead worm to use as bait off the end of a pier by the lake where we were going to film. I then cast my rod toward a spot where I thought they might just be biting that morning. Much to my surprise and everyone around me, a few minutes later something started tugging on my rod. Balancing myself carefully on my heels, I reeled in my prize while the cameras rolled.

When the piece aired on a local television station, the producer received hundreds of calls from viewers. Everyone said that the woman in the piece couldn't have been Eileen Fulton, not dressed up like that and reeling in such a large fish. The callers demanded that the film be shown over and over, because they were convinced the director had dubbed a picture of me or had utilized a celebrity look-alike.

After a three-week run at the Playhouse, I returned to New York and began filling in my weekends with club bookings in the neighboring area. I even managed to squeeze in a four-week engagement starring as Lily in *Carnival* at the Club Bené, a New Jersey dinner theater, *while* I was doing *World*. Admittedly, I wasn't getting enough sleep, but I was happy and that always seemed to give me the added energy I needed.

I was also dizzy from all the whacks to the head I got every night. My leading man had to haul off and slap my face in a fit of anger, but because he was nervous about hitting me, I never knew where the blow would land. It often struck my ear, which frightened me because of a childhood ear infection. I tried to protect myself by covering the ear with the long wig I wore, hoping to soften the blow. The poor actor would get really tense, because he was a big guy and didn't want to hurt me. But his anxiety made him hit harder—unintentionally, of course.

We worked on it for days, trying to choreograph the slap. Nothing seemed to help. One night he actually lifted me off the floor with the blow. It hurt so much I couldn't stop the tears. I had a song that followed the scene, "I Hate Him," and that particular night I sang it with such intensity—because I was writhing in pain—I got more bravos than ever before. That was one run I certainly didn't want to extend. Years later, we met again. He's now one of my best friends and has become a brilliant night club director as well as a film producer.

Right after *Carnival,* I booked a flight to Miami Beach for five days. Dori came with me because she wanted to investigate a few possible nightclub engagements.

When we got to the airport, I didn't like the way the airline personnel talked about Amelia's quarters—the baggage compartment. I wanted her either with me or with the pilot. When they wouldn't cooperate, I switched airlines at the last minute. Thanks to Amelia, we were saved. The plane we were going to take was highjacked to Cuba.

When I arrived in Miami, I enjoyed five wonderful days of sleep. I knew I had another play to do as soon as I returned, so I took advantage of the beautiful weather.

After my brief vacation, I immediately began rehearsing the comedy *The Owl and the Pussycat.* I was especially looking forward to the show because the theater, Guy Little's "Little Theater on the Square" in Sullivan, Illinois, was one of my favorites. Tom Poston was playing opposite me and I always thought he was a funny guy.

We had only three days to rehearse, which was rough because it's a two-character play. Add to that the fact that the Hong Kong flu was attacking the city and you had two very uptight actors. When we started working together, I began behaving like a weird eccentric. I wouldn't eat out because I didn't want to expose myself to flu germs. For the first time in my life, I refused to touch money—fearful of the germs the bills or coins might be carrying.

I arrived at Tom's apartment one morning to rehearse our lines and was surprised to find a Christmas tree and his little girl opening her presents. I didn't even know it was Christmas. When I'm working on a play, I often forget everything around me.

Tom and I were scheduled to do the show for a week. I became crippled from the onset. We had a scene where we fight over the TV set. He tries to take it away from me and we pull at the television, a tug of war. During our struggle, Tom accidentally stepped on my foot. He knew he had hurt me, and in his efforts to help me he dropped the set. It crashed onto my legs, cutting through my dress and slip. I thought I would faint from the pain and spent my time between the second and third acts sitting with ice on my thighs to keep the swelling down. Guy Little, the owner and producer of the theater, raced to his home to get me clean ice cubes, because I was afraid to use ice from the theater kitchen in case it had a tinge of Hong Kong flu.

For the third act, Dori, who is a pro at stage makeup, did a great job of painting my legs, which were turning green and blue, with lumps beginning to show. By the end of the week I looked like I had four knees.

The night before we closed, I was standing in the wings next to Tom, but he didn't know I was nearby. I heard him praying: "Oh, dear God, please, please anybody but Eileen. Don't let her catch my Hong Kong flu."

I was so petrified I didn't even feel the pain in my sore thighs. The *only* person I hadn't avoided was now sick.

The next morning, we both had a fever of 104. Guy brought a doctor who gave us some shots and pills.

He said, "I don't know how you're both going to get through the show. I'd advise canceling."

No matter what—the show must go on. Guy had the doctor stand by because he was afraid we would collapse. We managed to not only get through but were deliriously funny. I don't remember any of it. We had two shows to do, back to back. During the matinee, there were a lot of people saying, "Take this. Swallow. Open your mouth."

During the evening performance, my shot of adrenalin arrived. Little Eva Norton, the girl who got the role of Sunny in *Sunny of Sunnyside* when I was a child, was in the audience. She brought me a beautiful long-stemmed rose. I don't remember much of it, but everyone said it was the best performance I ever gave.

One of the most wonderful things about becoming financially successful in any business is that it gives you the freedom to do wonderful things for the people you love. In 1968, when I had just turned thirty-five, I could barely control my excitement when I telephoned my parents and told them to start looking for a house they liked: I meant to keep the promise I had made when I was eight years old. One wintry Sunday afternoon, we were taking a ride, I remember, and I was in the backseat quietly dreaming, watching the purple streaks of twilight bleed into the horizon.

"Mama," I said, "when I grow up and become a movie star, I'm going to buy a beautiful house for us all."

Mother turned around, her pretty face magically lit by the setting sun. "Thank you, Sweetie. That would be lovely."

Daddy, being a preacher's son, never had a house of his own, and, being a preacher himself, he could never call his parsonage home. Mother is the only one of us who ever knew what it was like. In all the years with Daddy, she never owned furniture or had a choice about where to live—not that she ever complained, mind you. The one thing that was ours, in fact, was Mother's exquisite china, sterling silver, and sparkling crystal.

Several months after I made that call, Daddy telephoned to say they had located a beautiful piece of land in Black Mountain, North Carolina, with a brick ranch style house on it. I knew Black Mountain was a place they had always loved, so the next weekend I flew out and we surveyed the property. It was breathtaking. Through the house's picture window you could see a range of mountains, called the "Seven Sisters," majestically reaching up into the bright blue sky. I loved the view, the grounds, and the house, so I bought it on the spot!

Working on a soap means that you can do story lines that night-time television would never go near. Daytime can deal with more controversial topics, because when you're on five days a week, you obviously have more time to carefully develop a potentially volatile subject. The story of the illegitimate baby or the extra-marital affair—Lisa certainly had her share—can unfold gradually. There is time to show why a particular married woman is not getting along with her husband. Viewers can feel her loneliness and pain, so when she responds to the affections of a man who is kind and considerate, they are more likely to be sympathetic. In fact, soaps have a tremendously powerful effect on viewers. The *New York Times* once printed an article stating that during the period when *World* was really hot, in the early sixties to the seventies, people named their children Lisa and Bob more than any other name.

Of course, daytime television can be just as uptight and rigid as any other medium. Back in 1961, when I (Lisa) was carrying the baby who would eventually become young Tom, the CBS network censors would not allow me to say the word *pregnant*. I had to say "now that I am carrying Bob's child." I thought it just plain ridiculous! I was married to Bob and talking to my mother-in-law in the kitchen. We were doing our girl-talk thing and I thought it was so unnatural to say it the way they wanted. So I refused! The producers said, "You'll put us off the air!" Well, Ted Corday always said he hired me for my spunk, but I'm certain he got more than he bargained for.

"It's my scene and I'll say what I feel is right!"

"You can't! We won't allow it!" Ted echoed.

Anytime *anyone* tells me I can't do something, I just go nuts. Whether I really wanted to say the word or not was now beside the point. I felt backed up against a wall. The hours before we were about to go live that day were filled with tension. Everyone was waiting to see what I would do. I hadn't made up my mind and decided to wait until the moment. We started the show and the line finally came. I paused for a second, looked down at my inflated stomach, rubbed my baby-to-be, and said, "Now that I'm like this." Everyone breathed a collective sigh of relief. The dignity of daytime was preserved for at least another day.

Because Lisa was such a vamp, I got to play a lot of boudoir scenes. When I first married Bob we had to sleep in separate single beds, but that didn't mean you couldn't do a lot of provocative, imaginative things *before* you even got near the beds.

One of my favorite "sex" scenes occurred when I was with my boyfriend, Bruce Elliot, while I was still married to Bob. Bruce and I were entwined on his living room couch.

"Oh, Lisa," he whispered. "Don't leave tonight. Please stay with me."

"I can't," I replied, "I have to get back to little Tom." I had moved out of the Hughes family house and a baby sitter was taking care of my little Tom. Bruce and I kissed and kissed and began working up a sweat. Finally I picked up the telephone. I began telling the baby sitter that I wouldn't be coming home because "I had to sit up all night with a sick friend" while Bruce continued working his way across my neck and face and shoulders. Then I dropped the receiver on the floor. Bruce began to climb on top of me while a fierce storm featuring thunder, lightning, and a fan-induced gale-force wind raged outside the French doors as the camera cut away. Now *that's* a sex scene! It's enticing and erotic but leaves something to the imagination.

Of course, all that would change once the soaps really started competing in the flesh department, when hunks would flash their golden-boy chests and young women would hop around in little more than a G-string. Although I do think there's a place for nudity, it's not on daytime. I can remember a time when someone had to examine all the dresses and decide which ones were too low cut. Just a little flash of a V neck back then could send those censors into fits of perspiration. I was forever having to put gauze or flowers or God knows what over my cleavage. We could smoke and drink and carry on, but we couldn't flash a little flesh.

When my publicist started booking me for "in-store" appearances—autograph-signing sessions at local department stores—I realized how powerful Lisa had become. I was provoking the kind of crowd reaction usually reserved for rock stars. The first of these appearances took place in the television department of Gimbel's in Morristown, New Jersey. This was before the birth of mall appearances, which are so popular today. Dori escorted me—she went everywhere with me by now. Before we arrived, she telephoned the store manager and warned them to be prepared: Dori was convinced the masses would arrive, but I wasn't so sure. The manager assured us that they had handled many "star" appearances and everything was taken care of.

From the moment we arrived, we knew it was going to be complete chaos. People were lined up everywhere: in the parking lot, outside the doors, crammed in the entranceway, all surging toward the television department where I was scheduled to appear. The manager called in his security department, but they took one look at the crowd and telephoned the police for assistance. The throngs kept pushing toward the front where I was standing, until I felt like I was going to be devoured. I jumped on the table, partly to protect myself but mainly so the fans could see what "Lisa" was wearing. I looked down and saw a small girl standing in front of me with a kitten.

"This is for you, Lisa," she squealed. "She's Lisa the cat and I want you to have her."

The poor thing was getting crushed, so I begged the crowd to back up. Finally the police arrived and took control of the situation, but it was really quite frightening. I grew to love the tours—and the mob scenes. They're always a great gauge for one's popularity.

In the spring of 1970, Dori suggested I merge my popularity in television with my love of singing by making a record. She had a friend who said he knew of a wonderful record company called Pan Records, which focused primarily on developing new R&B artists. I thought it was a terrible name, but I decided to throw caution to the wind and meet with the company's manager. Who could have predicted that that particular wind would turn into a tornado which would keep me spinning for the next ten years?

Dori set up a meeting with Danny Fortunato, a handsome, self-assured Italian who would soon become Husband No. 2. My first meeting with Danny took place on a hot, sultry summer's day. Outfitted in a simple but stylish white silk dress, I rode the elevator to Pan's office with a great sense of anticipation. The moment I laid eyes on Danny Fortunato, I could feel myself starting to melt. Lurking beneath his ruggedly handsome exterior was a sense of adventure mixed with a little danger. I knew getting involved with a man like that would be one helluva ride, but I was prepared to buy a five-year pass!

I presented several scrapbooks filled with clippings to give Danny a sense of the kind of press I could generate. He sat back in his brown leather chair and carefully looked at everything. He was very cool, very strong, very self-assured. Danny smoked small black cigars and punctuated his page-turning by blowing a thin but steady stream of smoke into the air. I found the whole scene intoxicating and was ready to play Bergman to his Bogart the moment he fed me the right lines. He listened to my tape, carefully lit another cigar, and then announced that Pan would be very interested in signing me.

A few weeks later, Dori, Danny, and I met at the Mayflower Hotel on Central Park West to sign the contracts. I remember wearing a new Bill Blass creation. The fabric looked like lace on spun gold with pale pink and lavender flowers. I still have the dress—some twenty-five years later! We brought along a photographer to capture the moment. As the flashbulbs began to flicker, Danny leaned over and brushed two full Italian lips across my slightly small and trembling southern ones. My God! It was just like in the movies when all the fireworks light up the sky. I was knocked head-over-heels!

A week later, Danny and I started working on my album, *The Same Old World*. In addition to recording some standards, Danny hired several writers to work on original material for me. He was a wonderful record producer: Kind and creative, he loosened me up as a singer and taught me how to act a song as well as sing it.

"Eileen, you don't have to sing every note that's written exactly the way it's written. Sing with your whole body. Bend it, shape it, make it yours."

Musically, I owe him a lot.

The title song from the album was a rousing spiritual, gospel-type tune. We worked on the material in one of the rehearsal rooms at Pan Records on Fifty-fifth Street.

Because there was no air conditioning in the building and New York was enduring a particularly hot summer, we frequently kept the windows open. There was a parking lot adjacent to Pan. Whenever we flung open the windows to rehearse, the parking attendants would start to sing along. By the end of the week, they knew the chorus and had even worked out a few dance steps. It was such fun!

Danny would stand behind me and breathe down my neck. Everyone in the office would gather round, clapping and singing, "It's the same old world, the same old merry-go-round." With the parking attendants as backup, I was sure we had a hit on our hands.

Unfortunately, when we went into the recording studio, the atmosphere was very different. It was ice cold and very sterile. The song lost its heated, sensual spirit. I guess we should have hired the parking lot attendants for the day.

One evening we went to dinner at Santa Lucia on Fifty-fifth Street. When I walked through the door I remembered I had eaten at the restaurant when I was a little girl living on Staten Island. My parents had invited me to join them and Emily Kalter, a wonderful opera singer. That was a very special evening for me and remembering it made me quite vulnerable. Danny and I talked for hours. I found myself casually brushing my fingers across his arm whenever I had to reach for something on the table. He had a strong, solid arm and I loved that. It was a gentle but very exciting beginning.

Danny was cautious with me because, as I later found out, he thought a "big star" would have nothing to do with him personally. And I was scared to death that he wouldn't want to become involved with me because I was well-known. I've learned it's not the easiest thing in the world being married to an actress who's always playing to the press or signing autographs on the street. It requires an individual who has a strong sense of his own identity, one who is secure and realizes that he is the "wind beneath your wings." It's taken me a lifetime to figure that one out.

I began to have a nagging feeling—encouraged by Dori—that Danny might be married. Dori told me that whenever she called his house, two different women answered the phone: The older-sounding one who couldn't speak English she felt was obviously his mother, but Dori thought the other, a younger, gentle-voiced woman, might be his wife! As it turned out, his mother had the soft and gentle voice and the one who couldn't speak English was his aunt.

All that summer I was terrified to ask him for fear that he might really be married. That fall, I went to Sullivan, Illinois, to do Neil Simon's *The Star Spangled Girl*. While Danny was on the road promoting records for Pan, he came to visit me. I insisted he stay at the "star" house where I was living—of course, we had separate rooms. Sullivan loved me—at least they did until Danny showed up. I had been there before, and they always looked upon me fondly, as if I were their little girl. It was almost like being the preacher's daughter again. The good people of Sullivan perceived that this dark stranger was soiling their princess. Neighbors would stare at me from their windows and then close the blinds. Danny and I would walk down the street, holding hands, and people would glare at us, no longer wishing me a pleasant "hello."

One thing's for sure: a little scandal certainly didn't hurt business. The theater was packed every night, because everyone wanted to see this "bad" woman. Danny and I always maintained a sense of propriety. I admit we necked like crazy, but we weren't doing what everyone thought we were. It was our secret, which made it a lot more fun and exciting to hold off.

There were early signs that Pan was not the perfect record

company for me, but I turned a blind eye because I was swept away by my feelings for Danny. When the time arrived to release my debut album, however, something frightening occurred that even *I* couldn't ignore. CBS was going to help me promote *The Same Old World*—their publicity department had finally changed that "we don't work with the soap stars" policy. They sent one of their reps to Pan to pick up several boxes of albums. When the young man arrived, he found that the office had been padlocked. There was a notice from the sheriff preventing anyone from entering the premises. I was horrified to think that all the hard work I had done was about to go down the tubes. Through a lot of legal maneuvering—and money from the "La Fulton" savings account—I eventually got my albums.

We later found out that the president of Pan was sitting at his desk with a machine gun on his lap when the CBS rep arrived. He was prepared to shoot anyone who came through the door! The company quickly folded, but I believed Danny when he said that he didn't know anything about the entire fiasco.

Everybody seemed to be against my relationship with Danny—especially Dori. I'm certain she thought he was just using me and that eventually she would be replaced. All of the opposition just made me love him even more. It brought out the rebel in me—even though it wasn't in my best interest. I took Danny to the studio one day, and although the cast and crew were kind, I could see my swarthy Italian was a bit rough around the edges compared to these savvy, sophisticated New Yorkers. His clothes weren't quite right, his tie was the wrong width, but I didn't care. When you're in love, who cares about fashion? I was so nuts about the guy, I even switched from the Mets to the Yankees, his favorite team.

Danny had that old-fashioned sensibility which makes me weak in the knees: He loved to hold my chair, open the door for me, stand up when I entered or left the room. Dori kept saying, "Sleep with him, have an affair, get it out of your system. But for God sakes, don't marry him. It will be for all the wrong reasons."

In September 1970, Danny proposed to me at the Santa Lucia, the restaurant where we had our first unofficial date— where I first brushed my fingers across his arm. I immediately accepted, but no wedding date was set. He began staying at my apartment more and more, and by November I knew he was there for good. I came home from the studio one day and saw his baseball bat leaning against my piano. That's what he brought with him into the marriage: a baseball bat. I suppose it was a bad omen, but I didn't see it then.

I loved coming home after a long day at the studio to find him there. He would pour me a glass of wine and I could smell the spaghetti sauce cooking—he was a marvelous chef. The whole romance of living with someone you love is overwhelming. But when I came in that day and saw the baseball bat I remember thinking, *Oh, my God, this is for real!* Then I felt a stab of guilt and considered having it mounted and hung over the piano like a prized fish.

I was happier than I could have possibly imagined. My days were filled playing the scheming vixen Lisa and my evenings and weekends were devoted to the role of the "hopelessly lovestruck fiancée." My musical collaboration with Danny culminated in the release of a very successful 45, "Radio."

I was always very aware of my celebrity status when I was with Danny, but worked hard to ensure that he never felt like a background character. Whenever possible, I pushed him into the limelight—an area toward which he naturally gravitated. Whenever I gave interviews, I constantly brought him up, until finally my publicist told me that he was starting to get some negative feedback: Journalists who came to interview me said they were interested in the Eileen Fulton story—not in Danny Fortunato.

I was having such fun on *World* with the Lisa/Michael Shea story line—one of my all-time favorites. Lisa had had a wild affair with Michael, which produced a baby. Of course, Michael wouldn't have anything to do with Lisa or the child. He went off and married the respectable Claire and became a big-shot doctor. When the little boy grew up and Michael saw his child, he realized he now wanted to be the boy's father. Claire disappeared into soap opera purgatory. Eventually, Michael blackmailed Lisa into marrying him to get his son back. She had to agree to be the loving, faithful wife in front of everyone. Privately, however, Lisa made her new husband suffer.

I got to do marvelously bitchy things, like setting a beautiful table and cooking an elaborate meal. When my hard-working, hungry husband walked through the door, I'd lovingly announce, "Welcome home, darling. I've been slaving over a hot stove all day just for you." And then I'd serve a three-course dinner consisting of everything he was allergic to!

The bedroom scenes were the most fun: I'd wear a slinky negligee and get Michael all hot and bothered, whispering, "You're so sexy and attractive." I'd seductively open my gown and just when he was "ready," I'd cover myself and laugh, saying, "If only you were a real man!" It was such fun making him suffer. This was the Lisa the audience just loved to hate.

In the spring of 1971, Danny and I went to visit my parents. I wanted them to meet the man I was going to marry. We slept in separate rooms—but it was difficult to stay away. We were engaged, of course, but my daddy didn't know we were living together. You just didn't do that back then and flaunt it in your parents' face—at least not if you were a preacher's daughter. Finally, at the airport, I told my mother, "You and Daddy are welcome to come up and visit me anytime, but I want you to know that Danny and I are living together." I didn't know how she was going to react. Mother looked me straight in the eye and didn't bat a lash.

"I thought so, Sweetie."

Well, it wasn't long after that that I received a telephone call from my father.

"Old girl," he began, "I don't like the idea of your living like that for all these months. You've got to make it *legal*. I'll come up and tie the knot myself."

I decided if I was going to be married by my father, it should be in North Carolina. Since I had already had a real wedding with all the trimmings when I married Bill, I decided to do something completely different the second time around. I wanted it to be simple but special.

"All right, Daddy," I said. "If that's what you'd like, we'll get married. But I don't want a traditional ceremony with all that wedding stuff. I want to do it outdoors, on the side of a mountain. And I'd like Mother to bake a cake. But no one is to know. Just the family."

"Well, old girl, if that's what you want, then that's just what we'll do."

Mother baked a four-tiered wedding cake, but she couldn't work on it in the main part of the house because when company came by they would see what was going on. My parents had a small apartment in the downstairs part of their house that provided the perfect location for my mother's top-secret work. I was so adamant about not having anything traditional, I told Mother I didn't even want white icing on the cake. She created a lovely pink frosting with delicate flowers framing the sides.

I wore a simple blue and white cotton dress, which I had worn many times before, with white sandals that laced up the legs. I wanted everything to be familiar. Daddy had chosen several suitable locations for us, and on the morning of our wedding, he gave us a tour of all the possibilities. We picked a lovely spot overlooking all of Black Mountain. My parents were pleased with our selection, because it happened to be the same place where Daddy had proposed to Mother.

Besides my parents, the only other guests were my Uncle Tokie and my two brothers, Jimmy and Charles. As Danny and I exchanged our vows, a soft, gentle rain began to fall while a cricket sang. It was far away from the kind of noisy, fast-paced life I had been living in Manhattan, and it was everything I wanted for a second wedding. Simple. Personal. Meaningful.

Everyone went back to the house for a glass of champagne and a piece of Mother's fabulous cake. During the party, Charles lit a fire. The smoke backed up into the house, but I didn't even mind, I was so happy to be with so many of the people I loved. We saved the top of the wedding cake to take to Danny's parents, who didn't really believe we were getting married. When they read it in the paper a few days later, they knew we weren't joking about our plans. When we brought them the top of the cake and they tasted it, Mama Fortunato said it had an unusual smoky flavor—from the chimney smoke! I laughed at the time, but hoped it wasn't going to be a bad omen.

I had kept the wedding a secret from everyone in New York, but gave the exclusive to Earl Wilson, one of the most popular celebrity columnists at the time. He published the story with a picture of me in my costume from Neil Simon's *Star Spangled Girl*.

"She's a bride!" proclaimed the caption over a picture of me outfitted in boots, mini-shorts, a push-up bra, and pig tails. Every magazine in the country ran with the news—and the picture. I took one look at the photo and hoped my fans wouldn't think that was what I wore to the wedding!

After a very short honeymoon, Danny and I rushed back to

New York because I had to go back to work. I had that post-marital glow and loved sharing all of the wedding details with my soap family. I really felt like I had it all: a fabulous job, people I enjoyed to work with, enough money to support myself and look after my parents, a wonderful apartment, *and* the man I loved! However, I hadn't even been back a day when my bubble burst.

We were in the rehearsal hall. People were reading through other scenes, and I was quietly reviewing all of the congratulatory fan mail I had received since the announcement of my marriage. I was in a very euphoric state. But then I slowly began reading a letter that made me feel dizzy—like someone was jabbing pins and needles into my body. It was from a woman who had seen the picture of "Mr. and Mrs. Fortunato" in the newspaper. She said that Danny was *her* husband and that they were still married!!

I wanted to let out the kind of wail usually associated with Greek tragedy. Was this some crank letter? A jealous fan? Or the truth? It played into the worst fear I had had since the beginning of my relationship with Danny—the fact that he might be married.

I was horrified and nauseated but didn't say a word to anyone at the studio. How could I tell a soul that my hero might be tarnished? I rushed home the second the show was over and ran into the apartment. As soon as I closed the door, however, I froze. What if it were true? I was devastated but didn't want to appear out of control. After taking several deep breaths I located Danny in the kitchen and began speaking so softly he could barely hear me at first.

"Am I Mrs. Fortunato? Tell me I'm really Mrs. Fortunato."

Danny looked puzzled.

"Please read this," I whispered as I extended the letter from my quivering hand. "Please tell me it's not true."

Danny slowly read the wrinkled sheet. "Oh, my God!" he cried. "Don't worry about it. I'll take care of it."

Let me give everyone a sage piece of advice: Anytime anyone in your life utters those three sentences—"Oh, my God! Don't worry. I'll take care of it!"—it's a sign that something is seriously wrong about which it is well worth the worry.

Unfortunately, I was too frightened to pursue the matter. I left the entire mess in Danny's hands and hoped he would be able to make all of our troubles and problems disappear.

And for a while, he did.

SIX ~

# THE SPOILS OF SUCCESS

*P*eople often ask me why I think soaps are so popular—as if there were some incomprehensible mystery that would explain why anyone would devote two to four hours a week following the adventures of a group of fictional characters. I always laugh and say, "What got the public hooked on Shakespeare or Dickens or the great radio dramas of the thirties and forties: love, murder, jealousy, infidelity, ambition, revenge—all real life situations being played out by characters who demand your attention. It's just that on a soap, one particular character might experience them all in a single month!"

No one questions why millions of people spend hours every Sunday watching a group of guys throw around a funny-shaped leather ball. Football fans devotedly follow the adventures of their team, week after week, living vicariously through their ups and downs. The way I see it, one man's soap is another man's sport. They're both forms of entertainment and both add a little excitement to life.

I didn't grow up watching a lot of television, but I did listen to soap operas on the radio. Whenever the story lines got really good, I used to pretend to be sick so I could stay home from school and follow the latest adventures. I loved *Our Gal Sunday* and *Stella Dallas,* but one of my all-time favorites was *Wendy Warren and the News.* Wendy did a real news cast, which was unusual for a woman at the time I was growing up. When she was finished, you would hear voices in the background carrying on a conversation as if they didn't know the microphone was still on. Wendy, her producer, and the crew would start talking about their personal lives, and before you knew it, they were off and running into the story line of the soap. It was a very clever idea—very voyeuristic.

One time our gal Sunday fell into a pit with a gorilla, but my mother wouldn't let me stay home to find out what happened next. I had touched the thermometer to the light bulb one time too many to get the mercury to rise: It shot up out the top, bounced off my bedroom wall, and splattered on the floor into a hundred pieces. Despite my many attempts to convince her, Mother refused to accept the fact that my fever was so high *it* had shattered the thermometer. She forced me to go to school that day, and I never found out what happened in that pit with the gorilla. When anyone talks about being hooked on soaps, I can definitely understand.

For years, many viewers—especially men—were ashamed to admit that they watched soap operas, which got their name from the many soap detergent companies who were the original sponsors. For a while, I even developed an attitude about soaps. The first time I quit *World,* I said in an interview, "I'm sick and tired of soaps. They're just too limiting and I don't want to play one character until I'm sixty. The whole idea is just plain stupid." Life has a wonderfully ironic way of making you eat your words.

A man from Long Island wrote to me when I talked about being "sick of soaps": "Dear Lisa: I've watched your show since it began and I take great offense to your attitude because I'm an intelligent person. I make a point of watching you during my lunch hour and your comments have insulted me as a viewer. I like the show and I think it's good."

Of course, I realized he was right, so I never talked like that again. It was insulting, not just to the medium and my own hard work but to everyone who watched the show—especially my fans. Whenever anyone insults or criticizes a particular type of show, whether it's a soap or a talk-show or even one of those tabloid journalism programs, they should remember that they're also attacking the viewers who support those programs. It might be more interesting for these critics to begin to explore *why* such programs are so popular.

Soap actors are not as highly paid as nighttime actors, and they certainly make less than film actors, but it's a living no one has the right to complain about and it's definitely more consistent. I always say I'm the best living example of job security as an actor. When Irna first created soaps, I think she had the mother-housewife in mind as a viewer. The original shows dealt with women's problems because most of the audience were women. Story line conflicts revolved around marital difficulties, child-rearing, in-laws, and the town. You certainly didn't have career women depicted on soaps when I entered the business. Thanks to Irna, we eventually started branching into the world of doctors and lawyers, which attracted a larger audience. The topics of conversation at Nancy Hughes's dinner table now included the problems of professional working people.

When I met and spoke with many of my female fans during the sixties, they told me their husbands watched, and got hooked on, our show when they came home for lunch. This was back in the days when the wife didn't work and the husband actually had time to drive or walk home at the noon hour. The women made it quite clear that if their mates wanted a cooked meal, the men would have to sit still and eat quietly while the women of the house watched their favorite program. There are very few individuals who aren't eventually drawn into the world of soaps if they're forced to watch for a month or so. Ask anyone who has been hospitalized or unemployed for an extended period, and you'll find a new soap addict.

For years, men were afraid to admit that they actually enjoyed watching shows like *World* because it might be a threat to their masculinity. In 1971, shortly after I had married Danny, I found out for the first time just how many of my fans *were* men when I traveled to Omaha to do my nightclub act. I walked out on that stage each night, amazed that there were more men than women in my audiences. I later found out they were farmers who listened to the show on the radio bands in their tractors when they were working the fields. They weren't ashamed that they enjoyed listening to a soap opera. And I can assure you, a punch in the nose is what anyone who dared tease this macho group of machine movers would have gotten.

I began to pay more attention to who the fans were: cabdrivers, salesmen, doctors, the telephone repair man—they all watched. During the sixties and seventies, *World* was the most popular soap on the air. People used to tell me that if you were hospitalized, it was impossible to get a nurse between 1:30 P.M. and 2:00 P.M. because they were all in patients' rooms glued to the set.

In the late seventies and early eighties, college students made soap addiction a socially acceptable ailment. Accordingly, producers and writers began creating more story lines that centered around young people. I was never surprised that we attracted a young audience. From my earliest days on the show I received piles of mail from children. Even though Lisa was a lying, scheming, conniving vixen, she was a good mother who would do anything to help her kids—that quality alone redeemed her. I have learned that viewers will accept and enjoy almost anything hateful and spiteful adults do to each other, but if a grown-up betrays a child, it's an unforgivable act—one that is certain to lead to the demise of the character. Children often wrote seeking advice about issues they couldn't discuss with their parents. They knew I would take them seriously and offer some motherly suggestions, so whenever possible, I tried to answer them personally.

I was convinced that college students watched soaps because they were homesick. If they turned on *World* and saw Lisa and Bob and Nancy, somehow they could connect to that familiar feeling they had watching every day back home. When you're in an unfamiliar environment or situation—a new job, home, or city—there's nothing more reassuring than turning on the television and being visited by your "old friends." Magazines wrote articles about this phenomenon. The media thought it was amazing—I didn't. I knew they just missed that sense of belonging somewhere.

With the dissolution of Pan Records, Danny no longer had a job. It's hard enough being married to a well-known television personality when your life is in order, but being out of work with no immediate prospects, made for a tense situation. I didn't want Danny to become a house-husband and have everyone start calling him Mr. Fulton. As a means of ensuring him a steady salary, I decided to let Dori go and to make Danny my manager. Dori continued to criticize and bad-mouth Danny after we were married. She also began to drink too much. She gained weight and started to take diet pills, and when she mixed them with liquor, her judgment and behavior were impaired. Of course, she had no idea the pills were affecting her. I know she felt like a third wheel and was fighting to keep me as a client—I was her only one—but she didn't handle it very well. If she was going to force me to choose between her and my husband, did she really think I would just walk away from Danny?

There was a lawsuit—isn't there always in cases like this? Dori felt I owed her a commission for a job in Georgia she secured while she was still my manager. Danny said I shouldn't pay, and, once again, I sided with my husband. But I was wrong. It was difficult facing her in court, and I regret the way I handled the situation. If I had just been smarter and talked to her, we could have been a happy family. Dori was totally devoted to me, but I was caught up with my new husband and couldn't see straight. I didn't speak to her again for over ten years.

And then in 1984, when I was celebrating a birthday and feeling alone, Miss Frankie suggested I call Dori to see if she wanted to work with me again.

"Eileen, she really cares about you and I'm certain she'd love to manage you again."

When I telephoned Dori and apologized, she was very gracious and kind.

"Oh, my dear, sweet friend, I wish I could help you, but I'm not well. I have cancer. I so often wanted to come and hear you sing at the different clubs, but I never went for fear of upsetting you. I've thought about you a lot and watched you on the show. Thank you. Thank you so much for calling. It means more than you'll ever know."

With Dori out of the picture and no one else around to influence my decisions, Danny took full charge of my career. We started working on another album. Danny hired a wonderful musical arranger named Howard Hodge. I adored him and wanted Danny and me to be like Howard and his wife, Donna. She was so beautiful and they looked so happy together. I thought they were the perfect couple. Perhaps, in retrospect, I wasn't the best judge of happy couples. Several years later, when Danny and I were driving home one night, we heard on the radio that a man had been murdered and it was plotted by his wife: It was Howard and Donna!

I was thrilled when I got a booking to do my nightclub act at the Persian Room in the Plaza Hotel. It was one of the most glamorous show rooms in New York, with a fabulous stage and a dance floor. Eartha Kitt and Lena Horne used to sing there. It's since been turned into a dress shop, but I hope one day someone will restore it to its former glory.

Danny served as my musical director. He put together a twenty-one-piece orchestra for the occasion. I was the first soap opera performer to appear there, and I wanted to make a big impression.

Mother and Daddy couldn't attend the opening—Daddy wasn't well—but Uncle Tokie came with his new bride Mildred. I remember that to get to the stage you had to walk through the kitchen, past huge stacks of pots and pans and vegetables. I wore a gorgeous sequined gown for the opening night, and I had to dodge the waiters with their plates of steaming food as I approached the stage. I really was petrified that first night. When I entered the room, photographers everywhere began madly flashing pictures. It was like fireworks on the Fourth of July!

I was in the early stages of my nightclub career and still learning the craft. *Variety* gave me a nice review, but the *Daily News* rapped me, saying, "tis a pity she can't sing." I always read all my reviews. I like to know what people are saying about me—even if I don't always like it.

One evening I was in my suite at the hotel, putting on my makeup, when I heard this fabulous trumpet wafting in through the open window—it sounded just like the arrangements from my nightclub act. I thought, *That's my song he's playing, and in exactly the same key that I sing it in.* The street musician must have finished, because I heard a round of applause. When he began his next song, I knew something was up because it was the next song I sang in my act. Danny and I leaned over the railing and recognized one of our musicians playing on the street. He had on his tuxedo shirt and his jacket was folded in half, resting under a small hat with bills inside. When you're a musician, I suppose you can always use a little extra cash.

Danny and I went to Los Angeles to meet with Grant Tinker, the producer of *The Carol Burnett Show*. I wanted to try to convince him to have me as a guest on her show. It was an awkward meeting, because a few years earlier, I had pitched an idea that they ended up using—but not with me. In 1968 or 1969, I was hanging out in the CBS press office with Gene Schrott and Dori. I told Gene that I really wanted to do a nighttime appearance on a musical variety show like *The Carol Burnett Show*. Gene and Dori thought it was a fabulous idea, and the three of us began brainstorming about what I could do on the show. I can't remember if it was Gene's or Dori's or my concept, but among the three us, we came up with an idea that became one of Carol's most popular reoccurring skits: "As the Stomach Turns"—an obvious parody of *As the World Turns*.

"Now, Gene" I said revving up my comedic engines, "I could go on her show and play someone sweet and she could play the lying, scheming, Lisa-type character." Gene knew Carol because she used to live down the street from him in Scarsdale. He wrote a wonderful letter outlining our ideas and had it delivered to her home, but he never received a response and I never appeared on her show.

Irna got really peeved when the skit became so popular, but Proctor & Gamble convinced her it was the highest form of flattery. It certainly helped put our show on the map! But when Danny and I met with Mr. Tinker, he wasn't very receptive to our ideas. I thought the press would have had a field day with Lisa appearing in an episode of "As the Stomach Turns" or swinging out on stage and doing the famous Burnett Tarzan yodel, but it just wasn't meant to be.

For a while Danny and I seemed to be happy. He traveled with me wherever I went, and we worked on projects together. In addition to putting him on my payroll, I gave him pocket money and an American Express card. I didn't want Danny to feel as if he had to ask me for money if he needed to buy something. I would say, "This is just a loan until your ship comes in" so he wouldn't feel like his pride was hurt.

Although there were minor flare-ups, harsh words, and temper tantrums, I always turned a love-struck-blind-eye toward Danny's "fits." I was learning he had an uncontrollable temper. One day, however, he did something I could no longer ignore: He treated my father—the man I loved, admired, and adored—in an insensitive and disrespectful manner.

Daddy had suffered a minor heart attack, so we drove down to see him. I don't think Danny wanted to visit my parents. He certainly made no effort once we arrived. It seemed as if he was going out of his way to behave in a surly way toward my father—which he had never done before. He came to the dinner table bare-chested. Mother politely asked him to put on a shirt. He returned a few minutes later with a Brando-like tattered T-shirt that was hardly an improvement. Mother was just flabbergasted.

A few days later, when we were getting ready to leave, he expected my father to load the bags into the car. I was completely embarrassed. When I asked Danny to carry the luggage, reminding him of my father's illness, he looked at me with a kind of hatred in his eyes that just took my breath away!

I couldn't understand what was happening—why he was so hostile. Perhaps my devotion toward my father made him jealous. Danny didn't like the idea that anyone—besides himself—might have my sole attention or be in a position to influence me. At that moment in time, however, Danny was not the center of my universe—my father was—he needed my love and attention. Danny didn't see it that way, and we fought the entire drive home.

After that unpleasant visit with my parents, I began to perceive everything about Danny in a new light. The veil of charm had been lifted. I was no longer blinded by my love for the man. Unfortunately, I was so busy working at my career that I rarely noticed what was really happening to my marriage. It seemed to me that the harder I worked and the more money I made, the more my marriage began to deteriorate.

Everything in our life got bigger—but not necessarily better. We added more singers and dancers to my nightclub act, which cost a lot of money. We moved into a large three-bedroom apartment in the then new ASCAP building on Broadway. Danny wanted a house, so a suitable dwelling was purchased in New Rochelle. He even switched from his customary cigarillos to large, thick Cuban cigars.

Even *World* got bigger: We went from a half hour live to an hour on tape. The studio graciously provided its "star" with a limousine and a driver to transport me to and from work each day. Danny felt threatened by Andy, my ruggedly handsome chauffeur, but I felt protected: I was starting to get death threats!

Some of the viewers took great exception to Lisa's manipulative efforts to get Bob back. One particularly distraught individual from Connecticut wrote to Bob Stanton (then president of CBS) and the producer and writers and said, "We're going to find her and we're going to make it so that she can't work anymore." The network took the threats seriously: They hired police guards to walk me to my car, and I always had a bodyguard whenever I did personal appearances. Stalkers have had a disturbing influence on the lives of actors in recent years. One actress on a rival soap was so frightened that she quit her show and went into hiding!

Just before our show expanded to an hour taped format, the technicians decided to go on strike. The multimillion-dollar business of television, however, stops for no one. The producers recruited anyone they could find—office workers, writers, even one of the receptionists—to run the cameras and booms (a boom is a microphone that is attached to the end of a very long pole, which in turn is attached to a heavy pedestal on wheels and is rolled from one set to another). Although it was a valiant effort on everyone's part, it quickly turned into a comedy of errors.

I was sitting in Lisa's living room, getting ready to do a serious scene with Bob's brother and watching the fight scene that was taking place just across from me when I noticed that the boom mikes were not in place—the actors couldn't be heard! Suddenly I heard someone to the left of me scream, "I got it! I got it!" At the same time, one of the secretaries who was working a boom mike on the other side of me yelled, "I'll do it! I can get there!" Both sets of boom operators began racing toward the scene and crashed into each other. The viewers at home saw a fight taking place, but instead of the correct dialogue they heard the screaming boom operators.

The next scene was in a bar. One of the actors was seated on a stool, and to emphasize a dramatic point he stood up. Unfortunately, the gentleman operating the camera didn't know how to pan up to the actor's face (you have to squeeze the handles on either side), so when he tried to adjust the angle, he got a huge close-up of what is probably still the best crotch shot in the history of daytime television! The dialogue continued, but all you saw was a bright and shiny zipper. Finally everyone in the vicinity came from the sides and literally picked up the camera to angle it up to the actor's face. After that, the director instructed the actors to either sit or stand during a scene until the strike was over.

Dennis Cooney and me
rehearsing our very
first nightclub act.

Me and my boys—my
back-up dancers, that is!

(All photos unless otherwise noted are courtesy of Eileen Fulton)

Happy
Holidays

Eileen and Danny

I sent this Christmas card
to all my friends and fans.

My "fat" suit for the
first act of *Plaza Suite*.

This is how I looked when the audience thought I had let myself go.

This is how I looked in the second act of *Plaza Suite* after my "crash diet."

Performing "It Had to Be You" with Ray Stuart just before I twisted my leg and couldn't move.

All my children, Cici and Lala.

My wedding photo with soap husband Grant Coleman,
played by James Doug.

The day I left my lovely home in Connecticut to move back to Manhattan.

Husband number 3, Rick.

All decked out for a costume ball on *ATWT.*

Burt Reynolds dropped by the CBS studio and caught me with my hair in curlers. *(Courtesy of Andrea Ross)*

Two different faces and hairstyles of Eileen Fulton.

The *ATWT* cast photograph. I'm seated in the first row, second from left.

During the seventies, I continued working at my usual frenzied pace: Weekdays were spent taping *World,* weekends were filled traveling around the country performing my nightclub act. Danny and I continued to work on records, and I began to promote a new line of clothing for J.C. Penney's. When I look at all of the celebrities currently promoting products on the shopping channels, I realize that my line of clothing was a revolutionary concept at the time. Betsy Halpern at Celanese came up with the idea: She thought that since my character had broken up so many marriages by behaving in such a seductive manner, I should put my name to a line of beautiful, sexy, and affordable loungewear. I thought it was a fabulous and fun project. Shortly thereafter, the "Eileen Fulton At Home Collection" was born.

I selected the outfits and colors and wore them on the show, at home—everywhere! Can you believe I still have several items from the collection hanging in my closet! We traveled every weekend for ten weeks, performing large and elaborate fashion shows in malls across America. Danny loved charming all the women—and they certainly loved him. When he was in a particularly playful mood, he would model some of the robes, which made the women scream with laughter. He looked especially fetching in a pink valour number, puffing away on one of his huge cigars. The line sold for several years and proved to be very lucrative.

Danny's behavior began to grow more erratic and irrational: Sometimes he was the kind and loving husband, other times he was like a mad dictator. It's often difficult to look back and find that first loose thread that, when tugged through years of a marriage, unravels the relationship. Perhaps Danny felt a growing inadequacy living in the shadow of his wife's fame. His mother's constant disapproval of his career choice—she wanted him to be a doctor—may have contributed to what appeared to be his lack of self-esteem. Something dark was growing within him, and it began to vent itself in frequent and inappropriate ways.

I was putting in very long days at the studio—getting up at 4:30 A.M. and sometimes, not getting home until 8 P.M.; I would find the kitchen a mess. Since I didn't have the energy to prepare dinner, I finally suggested we hire a cook.

"Look, Danny," I said, "I'm tired and I've got a big show to do tomorrow. I can't keep up with this anymore. Let's just hire someone to help us."

He used my suggestion against me for weeks, performing his "My Wife is a Spoiled Star" routine for anyone who would listen: "My wife is a star, you know. She has a limousine pick her up and bring her home. She has a chauffeur, she has someone fix her hair, make her clothes, and organize her life. But now she tells me she needs a cook. So I say, 'Okay, if you need a cook, go out and get yourself a cook.' So what does my star do? She puts an ad in the newspaper. But who does she hire? A woman from Barbados who's not a cook at all. Her only qualification is 'I can read a recipe.' "

I fought with Danny about Dorothy, the cook I had hired, for weeks.

"I like her!" I declared. "She cooks what I want to eat. She's not an Italian or a German cook, but that's not what I need, Danny. I don't want fattening food. I want chicken, vegetables, and a healthy meal. And Dorothy can do that!"

He didn't agree.

Dorothy was kind and good and treated me like gold. She began to see the terrible fights we would have at the dinner table. I couldn't understand exactly what had changed. When we sat down to eat there was no toasting each other with an "I love you" or an "I missed you." Instead of partners for life, we had become opponents in an unpleasant situation.

One evening we were driving home and I saw a child struck by a hit-and-run driver. I begged Danny to follow the van and try to get the license plate number. He became so enraged he actually pulled to the side of the road and turned the car off. Danny didn't like to be told what to do. We sat in silence for several minutes. I was terribly upset and frightened. He told me quite emphatically that it was none of my business and that all I needed was a good meal.

We drove to an Italian restaurant. When I tried to convince the waiters to call the police—explaining I had just seen a child hit by a car—Danny told them in Italian that I was crazy. I didn't speak Italian, but I got the gist of what he was saying. He ordered me a stiff drink, which knocked me right out, then he dragged me back out to the car and began speeding down the highway. I didn't know if he was trying to frighten or punish me, but we were almost hit by another car. I even thought for a moment he was trying to kill me.

"Danny, please slow down," I begged. "That car just missed us. I'm in the death seat. I could have been killed."

My husband stared straight ahead as if he were hypnotized. "I don't care," he whispered and then floored the pedal once again.

When I look back now, I can't believe I let such things go on. It's embarrassing to think I could allow myself to be treated so horrendously. You want your dreams to come true. You want your life to be perfect. You want to be happy. So you try for as long as possible not to believe what's really happening.

Danny, who once inspired me to sing, now began to terrorize me during our recording sessions, blowing smoke in my face and humiliating me in front of the musicians. One time we were out on Long Island recording "Some Dreams Never Come True." Danny was just wild. He kept blowing that Cuban smoke in my face and I couldn't breathe.

"Again! Again!" he growled. "And do it better. And keep your fucking mind on what you're doing."

I wanted to run out into the highway and kill myself. I couldn't believe he would treat me like that. I wanted to bolster his ego, and instead I ended up sacrificing mine.

As our personal life continued to fall apart, so did our professional relationship. We were seriously in debt because Danny had tapped the resources of our joint corporation, Danleen, to finance a television project: a musical variety special that would capture my nightclub act for my millions of fans across the country. Danny wanted the best of everything for the television show and went hundreds of thousands of dollars over budget, working in a medium in which he had little expertise. The stress of his inadequacies must have caught up with him, because he continued to vent his frustrations on me.

It was a few hours before we were going to tape the show in front of a live audience. Nothing was working. Danny repeatedly stopped the rehearsal and screamed at me, calling me a "fucking fool." I was overworked and overtired, and finally had had enough abuse. I became very still and looked him dead in the eye.

"Don't you ever, *ever* talk to me like that again!"

I couldn't believe I had finally stood up for myself. Danny stormed out, shocked that I was capable of speaking to him like that.

I had two hours to get ready for the show, but Danny refused to take me back to our rented apartment. George Bunt, a dear friend, the choreographer of our show, said he would take care of me. I just broke down and cried. Two hours later I was singing and smiling in front of hundreds of adoring fans. Whether it's Broadway theater, live television, or a misconceived, over-budget television special, the show must go on. After that, I lost my enthusiasm for singing.

My physical relationship with Danny—which used to have more rocket power than a launch to the moon—was grounded and in a state of indefinite delays. I began to suspect other women and finally went with my parents to visit a lawyer, seeking advice on what to do about my failing marriage. It was a stressful period, trying to determine if there was anything left worth salvaging.

I was feeling very fragile, and a kind word or act from a stranger could reduce me to tears. One evening Danny and I went to dinner with some friends from Minnesota. I went to the ladies' room and a woman stared at me and smiled.

"Aren't you Lisa?" she asked like a little girl who was about to get her favorite wish.

"Yes," I answered. I tried to be polite, but I felt so despondent.

"I can't believe it. I love watching you. But didn't you used to sing? I loved your voice. Why don't you sing anymore?"

It suddenly occurred to me that I hadn't sung for a very long time. I hadn't done a lot of the things I loved for a long time. I sat in front of the mirror and looked at a sad woman—at myself—staring back. Suddenly I flashed to the last time I had really looked at myself. I had said good-bye to Bill and had rushed to the theater to get ready for my show. I remembered staring at myself in the mirror then, wondering what I would do next.

*I used to be a person,* I thought. *I used to be me. What happened?* I completely fell apart.

When I returned to the table, it was obvious something was wrong. Danny was visibly irritated. One of our guests kindly offered to escort me outside for some fresh air. I had never talked to anyone outside of my family about my marriage, but suddenly I found myself confessing.

"Danny doesn't love me anymore," I sobbed uncontrollably. Just saying it out loud was shocking to my ears. I said it again just to be sure I meant what I said. My friend listened attentively, acting more as a father confessor than a counselor. After a few minutes I decided to reveal something I hadn't even told my parents: "I think my husband wants to kill me." Danny had recently taken out a very large life insurance policy on me—of course I was paying the premiums—naming himself as sole beneficiary.

I seriously began to fear for my life.

Sometimes things can't get better until they get a lot worse. That certainly proved to be the case with Danny and me. In the winter of 1979, I couldn't take it anymore—I didn't know if he loved me, hated me, or simply wanted me dead. I was finally pushed to the brink of suicidal despair. One evening we were having a drink before dinner. During our conversation, Danny misunderstood something I said. It was so trivial I don't even remember what it was. But it instantly transformed him into a demon. He froze and just stared at me with an intense and all-consuming hatred.

"What's the matter, Danny? Please, please talk to me," I begged.

He continued to stare at me without speaking—as if he were in a hypnotic trance.

I was overtired, distraught, and on the verge of a breakdown. It really was more than I could take. I jumped up crying and ran out the door in my bathrobe. It was in the middle of winter, snow was drifting down, everything was white and quiet outside. I ran into the street and began screaming, "I want to die, I want to die! Please, God, let a car come by and hit me!" I had probably seen one too many Susan Hayward movies. In retrospect I think that what I really wanted was for Danny to follow me, notice me—save me. Suddenly I realized I was freezing—my feet were turning blue and frostbitten in my slippers.

I realized right there in the middle of that snow-covered street that I would have to save myself—and soon.

# SEVEN

# "Are You Going to Let Him Treat You Like That?"

*I*n the midst of my personal turmoil, I decided to hire a new press agent. I knew that if I ended up splitting with Danny, I would need someone who would be able to put my disastrous marriage in a positive light. Patsy Anne Pepper more than filled the bill. She had flaming red hair and a voluptuous figure. Patsy loved to wear dangly jewelry, which always rattled when she talked—which was all the time.

She found being in the middle of my breakup with Danny exciting, which should have made me think twice about her from the start. But I was drawn to her energy and enthusiasm. I eventually began to wonder if she was having an affair with my husband. The three of us would frequently have dinner together. I had reached the point where I was uncomfortable being alone with Danny. He would drive her home and not return until three or four in the morning.

One time Patsy invited me to a dazzling party for UNICEF. The party took place aboard the newly refurbished *Normandy,* docked in the Hudson, and it was a star-studded affair, with wall-to-wall celebrities, politicians, and photographers to capture every moment. I must have had my picture taken a hundred times that night and was glad finally to be left alone. Patsy insisted I take a picture with the ambassador to Israel who was expected to arrive at any moment. Right in the middle of dinner, she snapped her fingers at me.

"Eileen, come on now. He's over there. Let's do it."

"C'mon, Patsy, I just started eating. Can't we do it later?"

"No. Now's our chance. Over there. Go."

I gave in and sauntered over toward the gentleman I thought she had been pointing to.

"Hi, darlin'," I twinkled, turning on all of my southern charm. "My name is Eileen Fulton. I've been on television a long time and these people are going to take our picture. Now you just relax." The ambassador gave me an odd look. When he turned his face to the side and I saw his chiseled features, I chirped, "You've got such a cute profile, you should think about a career in show business—you might just make it one day!"

Everyone at the table started looking at me like my dress had just evaporated and I was standing there stark naked. I didn't know what was going on. After a few minutes, the ambassador asked me to sit down. I had charmed him and put him at ease and fulfilled Patsy's request for the requisite photograph. Mission accomplished! I was ready to push on.

"No, sweetie," I replied as I patted his cheek. "I'm going over there to see my boyfriend, Hugh Downs. He's sitting at the next table."

"You'd rather sit with Hugh than with me?" he asked incredulously.

"Well, of course. But you just relax and I'll come back if I have time."

The moment I walked away from the table, everyone began grabbing my arm. They were excited, awe-struck, and clamoring at once. "You've got real chutzpah talking to him like that!"

"Oh, c'mon," I replied. "I was just trying to make the ambassador feel at home."

"That wasn't the ambassador," one of the guests exclaimed, "that was *Robert Redford!*"

I thought they were teasing me. "Oh, go on home and wash your hair, I'm not falling for that! I know Robert Redford when I see Robert Redford."

Someone finally pointed out the ambassador, who was seated at the captain's table on the other side of the room. I looked again at the gentleman with whom I'd been conversing and realized I had made a huge Hollywood-sized mistake. The last time I could remember seeing Mr. Redford was in *Jeremiah Johnson* when he had a beard. I don't know what I was thinking.

I never saw or spoke to him again, but whenever I see one of his films I always think of the ambassador to Israel.

I didn't feel I could really talk to anyone about my marital problems with Danny. To save myself from going insane, I began to carry on long conversations with my Pekinese, Amelia Earhart (I had named my dog after the great aviatrix because I identified with Ms. Earhart's adventurous and independent spirit). If you've ever owned a dog, I'm sure you understand, but to anyone else it may sound crazy. I would ask Amelia for her advice or tell her what particularly horrible thing Danny had done to me that day. The amazing thing is she would talk back. Well, not so much talk, but babble. Amelia and I could go back and forth "conversing" forever.

I purchased Amelia purely on a whim. After my childhood dog, Micky, had died, I swore I would never own another dog. I was walking down the street with Dori one day, telling her it was silly that she had Sam, her Labrador, because he made it difficult to travel. As we passed a pet store on Third Avenue, I looked up and saw this funny-faced dog staring back at me. I had to go inside and find out what kind of dog it was. The moment I held the baby Pekinese, she just started licking my face. I broke down and bought her on the spot.

Amelia was very possessive. One day we were in the elevator of my apartment building. A nicely dressed gentleman smiled at her and said, "What a cute little dog." The moment he leaned over to pet her, however, my little lamb transformed herself into a lion: She bit him on the hand.

"Oh, my God. I am so sorry!" I cried. "I hope this won't turn into a lawsuit." When you live in New York or Los Angeles, have a recognizable face, and something goes wrong, it's always a potential lawsuit.

The man was very kind and understanding. "No, no, it's all right," he said. "I should know better."

A few nights later, I was at Sardi's at a pre-Tony Awards party. The room was packed tighter than my husband's Cuban cigars. I had just finished telling everyone at my table about Amelia biting the man's hand on the elevator, and then excused myself to freshen my makeup. As I pushed back my chair, I heard someone scream. When I turned around, I was horrified to realize that I had just crushed a gentleman's hand between the two chairs. I felt even worse when I looked at his face and realized it was the man from the elevator.

Before I had a chance to apologize again, someone at my table whispered, "That's Marvin Hamlisch. Eileen just crushed Marvin Hamlisch's hand."

I couldn't believe my bad luck. He was supposed to entertain the crowd that evening, but the way he was examining his crushed fingers, I wondered if he would be able to perform.

"Look, Miss," he began, "I'm going to try to play tonight if I can, but please, please, I beg you, don't get anywhere near me. Ever again! You are dangerous!!"

One time Danny and I were traveling to Peoria, Illinois, and the newspapers wrote "Eileen Fulton and her husband have arrived today in Peoria with their little Vietnamese adopted daughter, Amelia." I called the columnist up to laugh. "She's not Vietnamese, she's Pekinese."

Once when I was flying with another one of my dogs, Sarah Bernhardt, she became the reason that a stewardess threatened to have me incarcerated. Sarah loves to fly, but she hates the takeoff and landing. Her ears hurt from the pressure, and she screams like someone was poking out her eyes. I always carried her on and tried to keep her in my lap, because as long as I held her, she was fine. I was sitting in the first-class section of a 747 and asked my fellow passengers if they would mind if I put my dog in my lap just while we took off.

"Is anyone allergic? She won't cry if I can just hold her."

A handsome gentleman and his beautiful female companion seated directly in front of me were the first to agree. It wasn't long before the rest of the cabin concurred. I discreetly placed Sarah under a sweater in my lap, but less than five minutes later the stewardess found us out.

"You can't leave your dog there. It's against the law."

"But she'll scream and everyone around me doesn't mind. Please, it will only be for a few minutes." The other passengers tried to assist me in pleading my case, but the stewardess became indignant.

"I don't care. I won't have it. Now put that little thing back in its case or I'll have you thrown off the plane."

I put Sarah back under the seat in front of me. We managed to get through takeoff without going deaf. After we had been in the air for about two hours, I had to go to the ladies' room. When I returned to my seat, I saw the handsome gentleman who had been sitting in front of me on his hands and knees, rolling up and down the aisles playing with Sarah. He was talking to her in Italian and his companion joined in.

Our stewardess from hell—who looked like a Pekinese her-self—ran down the aisle.

"I'm going to throw all of you off the plane if you don't put that dog back."

"You can't throw us out at 33,000 feet," I stated in my best bad-girl voice, "or you'll destroy this plane. And think of that nasty draft. It'll just ruin that state-of-the-art hair thing you've got happening on your head."

"Fine," she declared. "I'll fix you. I'll have you all arrested when you get off the plane. You just wait."

"Go on," I urged. "Arrest us!"

Thirty minutes later, a small-framed gentleman walked up from business class. I watched him carry on a conversation with Sarah's playmate. Then he turned around to speak to me.

"Allow me to introduce myself. I'm Placido Domingo's lawyer—of course you do know that this is Placido Domingo your dog has been playing with, don't you?"

Celebrity Rule No. 1: Never admit to your own ignorance if you can help it. "Well, of course, everyone knows and recognizes Mr. Domingo."

"I don't think you can afford me, but I will represent you and your dog free of charge if you're all put in jail. And think of the publicity, my dear! It could be wonderful." The attorney went on to explain that the woman with Mr. Domingo was Tatiana Treyanos. They were en route to Los Angeles where they would be doing a concert together. Two hours later, when we disembarked, no one arrested us. The irritated stewardess just glared as we gathered our belongings and left. Her bark was definitely worse than her bite.

During the flight, Placido had invited me to attend his concert that evening. When we were collecting our luggage, he rushed over to me looking very distraught.

"Eileen, I have dreadful news!"

"What? What's the matter?" I asked thinking they must have lost or destroyed all of his luggage.

"I'm sold out! I just found out. There are no tickets to be had!"

I congratulated him and told him not to worry. "I'll just have to catch you the next time you're in New York." He thanked me for being so understanding, and, after exchanging a kiss on the cheek, we parted company.

By the time I had arrived at the apartment where I was staying, my secretary excitedly told me that Placido Domingo had just telephoned. A ticket was waiting for me at the box office, and he had invited me to attend the party afterwards. The concert was magnificent. Glorious music—glorious voices! When I walked into the party at Chasen's later that evening, Placido enthusiastically greeted me at the door by swinging me around and exclaiming, "But where is Sarah, my lovely Sarah!?!" He was such fun—and such a gentleman.

I knew things were bad with Danny, but somewhere in the back of my head I kept thinking, *Is it something I'm doing wrong? Am I making this up? Maybe I'm just misperceiving his behavior?* I wanted to be absolutely certain I had tried everything before I accepted the fact that there was nothing left to salvage. Despite many conversations with my family, my attorney, *and* my dog, Amelia, I still wasn't sure. It's funny how a total stranger can suddenly put your whole life in perspective in a matter of minutes. I got my best piece of marital advice from a woman who gave eye exams at the Department of Motor Vehicles.

I had decided to apply for a New York driver's license. Danny drove me to the office and stood in line with me, hovering, asking questions, drilling me with such intensity you'd think I was about to be questioned by the FBI. I reached the front of the line and the lady behind the desk began to administer the eye exam. I was nervous because of Danny's behavior. I could tell the clerk had been watching him and didn't approve of his attitude.

"Would you please read the top line?" she asked.

After I rattled off the correct letters, she asked me to read the third line.

Danny kept grumbling about the fact that this was taking too long. "I'm sorry, I have a bit of a headache. Could you wait a minute while I rest my eyes?"

My husband just exploded on the spot. "Goddamnit! Just read the fucking chart! How stupid can you be!?!"

"I can't," I cried. "My eyes hurt. I can't see it."

"Well, honey, it's no wonder," the clerk interjected. "Who *is* that man?" she asked, pointing a purple polished fingernail in Danny's direction.

"That's my husband."

"Are you going to let him treat you like that?"

"Like what?" I suddenly got defensive. Not so much for Danny, but I felt like if I agreed that he was acting horribly—and I put up with it—*I* was stupid. "Like what, like what," I repeated. "Just how is he acting?"

"That man is abusing you. Now the only question I have for you is are you going to stand for that? Are you going to let him hover over you and tell you what to do. Because if you do, you don't have my respect. And worse, you don't have any respect for yourself." She signed all the necessary papers without further administering the exam. "Here. Take this," she said, giving me the temporary license. "When you come back, I don't want to see you with *him*. And one last thing. Take a good long look at your life."

Someone else may have been offended by her presumptuousness—not me. I never went back, but I took her advice to heart. If a total stranger could perceive the situation so clearly, then surely I wasn't making it all up.

Despite the fact that we weren't getting along, Danny and I threw a huge Fiftieth Wedding Anniversary party for his parents in 1977. I organized a lavish and elegant affair for two hundred friends and relatives at the Fountainhead in New Rochelle. Mama Fortunato was so excited about the celebration—we spent weeks just discussing what she would wear (Danny's mother and I always got along very well). I let her borrow two fur pieces so she could look glamorous for the photographers. She absolutely loved playing the part of the "star" for a night.

After a lovely dinner, we spent what seemed like hours posing for the many photographers and members of the press who were covering the party. Later in the evening, approximately ten minutes after all of the press had left, a fight broke out. Glasses and fists were flying. Guests began to scream and run for cover. I couldn't believe what was happening. Apparently, Danny's Uncle Eddie got into an argument with his daughter's boyfriend. The boyfriend threw a punch and ended up severing an artery in his hand. There was blood everywhere.

That night, I was wearing a beige form-fitting dress with a matching coat trimmed in beige fox. I had been preparing to leave when the fight broke out, and though I tried to stop the men, no one would listen to me. Then the boyfriend bopped Danny's father on the head, escalating events even further. Danny was now furious. He had had a bit too much to drink and didn't hesitate to defend his father. He grabbed the young rabble-rouser, threw him to the ground, and held him down. Aunt Sophie began running in circles and screaming so uncontrollably I had to slap her to calm her down. It was rapidly turning into a nightmare sequence from a Fellini movie.

When I saw that Uncle Eddie was going to kick the boyfriend's head, I knew I had to do something. Without taking the time to remove my heels I jumped on top of the young man's stomach to block the kick (Danny was still holding him down), thrust my hands out like a mad policeman directing traffic, and yelled, "STOP!!!" Blood covered my dress and my feet. It was an absolute mess.

The police quickly arrived and began chasing the original troublemaker up a flight of stairs that led to a reception room where another celebration was ending. A young man was standing at the top of the staircase kissing his aunt good-bye when the troublemaker from our party flew into him, knocking him out cold. The police ended up arresting me, Danny, the boyfriend, Uncle Eddie, and anyone else who looked like trouble. They tossed us in the paddy wagon while Aunt Sophie collapsed in despair.

They drove us to a secured part of the hospital for criminals who need medical attention. Hours went by as they questioned everyone one at a time. I kept asking if the young man on the staircase who had been knocked out had been seriously hurt. His aunt, who was now seated next to me in a waiting room, kept staring at me.

"Aren't you Lisa? Aren't you the one on the soap?"

"Yes, yes that's the part I play," I answered.

"Well you're one of Stephen's—my nephew's— favorite actresses. He watches you every day. I can't believe it! You have to speak to him."

I asked the policeman and the doctor in charge if I could meet the young man and at least apologize for everything. They both gave me permission.

The moment I walked into the hospital room, I saw Stephen's face light up.

"Lisa! Lisa! I love you! You're so wonderful on your show! I can't believe it's really you."

"I'm so sorry for your trouble," I said quietly. "I didn't have anything to do with this, but I'm so sorry. Please don't sue me. What can I do to help you?"

Stephen's aunt said that if I gave them each an autographed photo—and Stephen didn't suffer a concussion—they wouldn't make any trouble. I told them I'd be happy to oblige them, and, escorted by one of New Rochelle's finest, I raced home and got the photographs that would undo the damage.

A few hours later, everyone was released. No charges were pressed. I wasn't certain if it was because of me (and Lisa) or if Uncle Eddie had called in a few favors, but I was relieved when it was finally over. The scandal never hit the papers because the press and photographers had left just minutes before the chaotic affair began! Can you imagine if they had been there?

As the saying goes, "Timing is everything in life."

I became increasingly concerned that something was physically or mentally wrong with my husband. His behavior could not be attributed to drugs or alcohol: The only substances he abused were Cuban cigars and me. Danny began to complain of severe headaches and, at one point, he thought he might even have a brain tumor. One time when he was on the road, he telephoned me from somewhere in Florida and didn't even know where he was or how he got there. Whenever I suggested he seek the advice of a doctor or psychologist, he just got angry.

I knew that if I was going to leave him I couldn't do it on my own. Two individuals proved invaluable in helping me plan my escape: Bob Sherwin, a family friend and the attorney who was already advising me, and Dr. Leah Shaeffer, a psychiatrist.

When my vacation was approaching in February 1979, both my attorney and psychiatrist advised me not to travel to La Posada in Arizona with Danny, which we had prearranged for months, because it was very isolated at that time. They were both seriously concerned that Danny's abusive behavior was escalating to the point where he might become a physical threat. I really believed it was just a matter of time before he started hitting me. He had already begun jabbing me and holding a fist to my face to frighten me.

My advisors suggested that I plan separate vacations—but not to tell Danny until the last minute. It seemed like a radical idea to me, but I felt I had to trust their advice. I got a different travel agent who planned a separate trip for me, separate tickets, separate limos to take each of us away. I managed to coordinate all of this without Danny finding out. I was a nervous wreck until V-Day (Vacation Day) finally arrived.

Danny was in a particularly black mood that morning, pacing around the living room, waiting for me. "C'mon, Scotty (his nickname for me because of my volatile Scottish temper), get your goddamn self moving and get in the fucking car, 'cause it's waiting outside. Goddamn your fucking slow ass, you stupid broad."

His language had deteriorated to that level. My heart was pounding so loudly I could see my blouse moving slightly: He would either go along with the plan or punch me in the face. I took a deep breath and tried to connect to that source of strength I tapped whenever Lisa had to play a particularly manipulative scene. "Danny, look out the window. That's *your* car."

"What are you talking about," he grunted.

"Look out the window. There are two limos. Do you see the one in front? That's for you. Do you see the other one two cars behind? That's mine. I've thought about this for a while and I've decided we need separate vacations, Danny. I'll be at La Costa but you can't come. There's no room for you there and you're not allowed, so don't try to follow me." I just made that part up, but he was so taken aback by my aggressive approach that he didn't question anything. Of course I had my driver-bodyguard to protect me in case Danny tried anything. Thankfully, he didn't.

Danny flew to Arizona and enjoyed a marvelous vacation courtesy of my American Express card. From the cost of his dinners, he obviously wasn't eating alone. When I returned from my well-needed rest, I was determined to end the marriage. I discussed the situation in detail with Bob and Leah. They both advised me not to be alone in the house when Danny returned. My brother Jimmy agreed to move in for a short period. When Danny finally returned, he walked in the door wearing a huge Indian headdress. He was tan and looked healthier and more handsome than I could remember. Danny seemed genuinely happy to see me, but the minute he noticed Jimmy in the other room, he just flipped out.

"What's *he* doing here?" he snapped.

"He's my brother and he's visiting me."

"I want him out of here!"

"No, Danny. He's going to stay for a while."

Danny took his bags upstairs and came running back down in a matter of minutes. He held two small identical boxes, one in each hand. After silently staring at me for about thirty seconds, he tossed the boxes in my lap, one at a time.

"One is because I love you, and the other is because you're sick!"

I opened them and discovered two identical silver and turquoise Indian bracelets. I didn't want a scene, so I went upstairs to bed. Thirty minutes later, Danny came marching in with a drink in his hand. From the way he was wobbling, I knew it wasn't his first. I was lying in our enormous bed, pretending to be asleep, but he switched on all of the lights and began marching around the periphery of the room like a caged animal. Suddenly he stopped. Although I felt like screaming and gasping for air, I made an effort to control my breathing and remain calm.

The worst possible thing would be to escalate the situation.

Danny balled up his hand in a fist and yelled, "What the fuck do you think you're doing having your fucking brother here?"

"Danny, he's just visiting me." I prayed to God he wouldn't hit me. I didn't take my eyes off of him but continued to stare him down. I kept repeating to myself, "I will not back down. I am not afraid." It was like two animals in the jungle deciding if one was going to attack the other. Danny kept marching around our enormous king-sized bed, spilling his drink and blowing smoke in the air.

"If you're going to drink, then drink, but please don't spill it on me," I stated in a calm, quiet voice.

He grew very still and looked straight ahead—not at me—as if he were hypnotized once again. His head snapped in my direction and he began shooting threats at me. "If that fucking brother of yours isn't out of here tomorrow, I'm going to kill his ass! I don't want him here. He's out. Tomorrow. Or else!" And then like a car running out of gas, he began sputtering, slowing down until finally he just passed out. I thought about making a run for it, but I didn't want to take the chance that he might wake up. I remained in bed, awake, watching the clock, until dawn.

The next morning, while I was getting dressed, Danny began repeating his threats. "If you don't get that fucking brother out of here, I'm going to kill him. It's *my* house. I promise I'll kill him."

I had had enough. A cold calmness embraced me like a shroud. "What do you mean *your* house?" I stated. It's *my* house and you will *not* kill my brother. If you continue to threaten us, I'll call the police!"

He was confused. Was I bluffing? Would I risk the inevitable bad publicity that might occur if I did call the police? This was a new, rational, aggressive, empowered Eileen—Scotty no more!—and Danny wasn't certain what I was capable of. When I headed for the telephone, he got so mad he grabbed his car keys, ran out of the house, and sped away.

"Jimmy," I called out, "this is it. Pack up. We're leaving. Now!" I tossed my credit cards, jewelry, and a hot water bottle into an overnight bag and drove into Manhattan. I would have left town, but I had a meeting with UNICEF and the March of Dimes, which I couldn't cancel, being spokesperson for both organizations. I walked into the lobby of the New York Hilton and asked to speak with the manager, who knew me.

"I'm checking in this morning, but I don't want anyone to know I'm here. I'll be using the name Ruth Stern and my brother will be Hillary Stern. Please don't put through *any* phone calls unless someone asks to speak with either Ruth or Hillary."

"Don't worry, Miss Fulton," he replied, "we do things like that more often than you would imagine."

I began to feel like I was in an extended episode of *World* and was ready for a commercial break. None came. I quickly telephoned my parents.

"I've left Danny. It's over. I'm not going to tell you where I am just yet, because I don't want you to have to lie. I know he'll call you looking for me. Don't worry, Jimmy's with me."

I also called my brother Charles and told him everything that had happened. It wasn't until the next morning that I telephoned my soon-to-be ex-husband.

"Danny, it's me. I'm calling to tell you I'm fine but I'm not coming back."

"You can't mean it!" he cried.

"I certainly do mean it."

"Please. No. Give me another chance. Come back. Please." He sounded desperate.

"Now, Danny, listen to me. I'm not going to tell you where

I am because I don't want to see you. That's it. It's over. I'll make arrangements to get my things later." And then I quickly hung up the phone.

The next morning Jimmy and I went down to breakfast. I didn't realize it at the time, but I was wearing a dress I had worn on the show a few days earlier. I no sooner walked into the restaurant than a group of tourists began screaming, "It's Lisa! Lisa's here and she's going to eat breakfast!"

Jimmy and I quickly assumed our chosen parts and began speaking in an Australian accent.

"What's that you say, love?" I asked using my best Aussie lilt. "I beg your pardon? I'm afraid I'm a bit foggy and can't quite catch what you're chatting about."

The spokesperson for the group told me in great detail that I could be the identical twin for a wonderful actress on an American soap opera.

"How terribly interesting," I said, trying to contain my laughter. "I've always heard there were people who have doubles walking about, but imagine having one who's an actress! Frightfully exciting!"

It took some doing, but we convinced them. They returned to their table very disappointed.

The next day Jimmy and I drove to Lake Minnewaska to relax and "hide" for a few days. We arrived on a foggy night, in the middle of a rain storm, complete with thunder and lightning. The shutters were banging and everything seemed to creak and rattle. Jimmy and I hadn't been there for fifteen years. It had certainly changed. Once we checked in, I saw it wasn't at all how we had remembered it. Dilapidated and run down, it wasn't the kind of restful environment I was looking for.

The next day, we drove to the nearby Mohonk Hotel, which was perfect. After a few days of rest, however, I had to get back to work. My first day I had to drive to Jersey for a location shot. We were starting a new story line that Doug Marland, our new head writer, had written especially for me. The first shot took place in a car. Lisa was driving in the middle of the night in a rain storm. She ran through the woods and found an old, run-down inn with banging shutters. I couldn't believe it! It was exactly what Jimmy and I had done! Doug was writing the scene as I was living it. Very strange.

I forgot that once I went back to work, Danny would be able to find me at the studio. He started to follow me and began hanging out in front of the studio entrance, hoping to catch me for a minute so he could beg for another chance. I tried to avoid him by dressing in wigs and costumes. I would put on a mustache, a pair of glasses, and a hat, and walk around the block to where my car and driver were waiting. Sometimes I would come out with the stagehands, dressed like one of the guys.

When I met with my attorney, I told him I wanted to give Danny half of everything—I knew I could have put up a fight to keep more, but I felt obligated to provide for him in some way. Danny kept leaving me messages at the studio, begging for a chance to talk to me face-to-face. After discussing the situation with my psychiatrist, I agreed to meet Danny one last time. She suggested Harry's Bar at 3 P.M. It was a safe, elegant restaurant where she was certain Danny wouldn't make a scene. At 3 P.M. it would be very quiet and we could talk in private.

I dressed carefully for the meeting in a black and white wool suit. I wanted to look like a businesswoman who was about to conclude a transaction. I rehearsed the scene many times in my mind, and although I was nervous, I was determined not to back down. When I joined Danny at the table, he looked so lost—so confused. There was a bouquet of flowers resting next to him on the bankette. I could tell from the crumpled state of the accompanying card that he had probably been waiting for some time, fingering the envelope in his anxiety.

"Danny," I began, "I decided to meet with you as a courtesy and to let you know where things stand."

"Please, *please,* give me another chance. Just one year. Come back for just one year and let's try to work it out."

"I'm sorry, Danny, but that's no longer possible."

"I can't believe you're talking like this! You're like a piece of ice. You have a heart of stone! Do you hear? Stone!! This isn't you. Someone's making you do this."

"Danny, no one is making me—"

"Please," he urged, his hands shaking slightly. "I'll do anything. I miss you. I miss everything about you. I'll be sweet. Really sweet. I'll try. Give me the chance."

And then he played his trump card: Danny quoted a line from a Katharine Hepburn/Sir Laurence Olivier movie called *Love Among the Ruins,* which we had once enjoyed when we were in love.

"Grow old with me, the best is yet to be."

I admit I was moved. For one fleeting second my hero emerged from the darkness. The one I loved desperately and I thought loved me. The one who would be the father of my children, the keeper of my secrets, a friend for life. I took a deep breathe once again and reminded myself that I had to move on. Despite the lack of patrons in the restaurant, I could feel the eyes of a few waiters and bartenders darting back and forth toward our table. I decided to cut to the end of the scene—the part I had rehearsed in my mind for hours. "Danny, where are your credit cards?"

"What?"

"Your credit cards, where are they?"

"In my wallet. What do you—"

"Please give them to me."

"What!"

"Give them to me. Now."

He was shocked, but too vulnerable to argue or refuse. While he emptied the contents of his wallet, from my purse, I removed a small pair of silver-plated scissors I had purchased especially for this occasion. At this point, the staff made no pretense about ignoring us: They were glued to the scene and couldn't wait to see what was going to happen next.

Slowly, deliberately, I picked up each card—the American Express, the Sears and Roebuck, the Visa—and cut it in two, enjoying the sound of the plastic as it landed on a fine china plate. I began to feel slightly dizzy, intoxicated by my liberation. But my sense of victory was quickly deflated by the sight of this helpless "boy" in front of me. You can get a divorce, you can "cut the cards," but you can't just cut ten years out of your life as if they never happened. I felt like a mother who had given birth to a monster-child and was now cutting the umbilical cord, setting both child and mother free to find their own way.

"I've paid all your bills, but as of today, you're on your own. You can stay in the house until it's sold or until you find a place of your own, but the bills there are now your responsibility. You can have half of the proceeds from the house and half of what's in the bank accounts. I'm not leaving you without, Danny—I'm just leaving you."

He began to cry.

If you are an empathetic individual—as I consider myself to be—it is impossible not to be moved by someone who is in such pain, even if that person has caused *you* pain. I desperately wanted to hold him and comfort him, but I knew I couldn't. I took one last deep breath and rose from the table.

"Bye, Danny. I wish you well. Be happy."

He gathered his courage and stood up, silently handed me the bouquet of flowers, and walked out the door. I breathed an enormous sigh of relief, exhausted by our encounter. I quickly paid the bill and left.

As I passed through the door that led to a small alcove, I spotted Danny hunched over in the corner—no more a threat but a crumpled, beaten man. Although he was facing the wall, I could see and hear that he was sobbing uncontrollably. He either sensed my presence or smelled my perfume, because he quickly turned around to face me one last time.

"Scotty, Scotty, please . . . please don't leave me . . ."

I stood frozen for a few seconds, staring, remembering, and wishing that things had turned out differently. But they hadn't. It may take me a while to get there sometimes—ten years with Danny—but I eventually make those choices, no matter how difficult, that allow me to move on, nudging my life forward in a more positive direction.

I walked out of the restaurant and got into my car. Danny followed me out, his body slightly twitching from the tears he was once again trying to hold back. As the driver pulled away from the curb and the car slowly joined the Fifth Avenue traffic, I watched Danny's face grow smaller and smaller, until I couldn't recognize it anymore.

Ironically, many years later, I was sorting through some of my legal papers when I found my marriage license to Danny. It was dated September 1980—not 1970. It wasn't even a valid license. A strange postscript to an even stranger relationship.

EIGHT ⌢

# MY BELOVED FANS

After terminating my ten-year marriage to Danny, I fell into an emotional slump. I still arrived at the studio each day with a smile on my face, but the minute I left, it was like flicking a switch: I just shut down. My friends and family were very kind to me during this period, constantly telephoning to make sure I was okay, and, in some cases, trying everything possible to cheer me up.

Someone even sent me a psychic to take my mind off my troubles. Perhaps she thought some fabulous news about what was just around the corner would lift my spirits. I was in a bad mood and didn't want a psychic. *I'm psychic enough,* I thought. *I don't need this.* But since one of my friends had gone to the trouble of calling the "Send-a-Psychic" company (check your Yellow Pages for the location nearest you) and had already paid for the visit, I decided I should be nice about the whole thing.

Two days later I made a pot of tea and started reading a magazine in my living room, waiting for my psychic to arrive. Just as I was halfway through an article describing the glamorous life of Jackie Collins, the concierge called up on the house phone.

"Miss Fulton, there is a gentleman standing at the desk who wishes me to tell you that 'your psychic has arrived.' "

"Yes. Yes. It's okay. Send him up. I'm expecting him." Wonderful, I thought. I'm sure the entire building staff is going to think that I'm so desperate after my last disastrous marriage that I need a psychic to tell me who to date. I decided to return to my article until the doorbell rang. By the time I finished the glitzy profile and began flicking through a photo shoot celebrating the new metallic colors for fall, I realized something must be wrong. Twenty-five minutes had passed. I telephoned the front desk.

"Hi. This is Miss Fulton. I'm so sorry to trouble you, but I seem to have lost my psychic. I mean, the gentleman you announced never got here."

"Yes, we know, Miss Fulton. He just returned to the desk. There seems to have been a mix-up. Don't worry, we'll direct him to the correct elevator bank."

I was no longer in a mood to read. I began pacing around the room, agitated by all of the confusion. Finally, the doorbell rang.

"What happened?" I asked without even properly greeting the man.

"I'm sorry. I got lost. I was on the other side of the building."

I wasn't in a forgiving mood. "What do you mean you got lost?!? You're supposed to be psychic. Couldn't you feel my vibrations pointing you in the right direction?"

"I'm already sensing a hostile aura which surrounds you."

I felt like saying, "You're about to sense a pot of hot herbal tea surrounding *you*," but I managed to remain silent. My previous comments certainly got us off on a bad track. After moving his palms through the air a few times—it looked like he was practicing T'ai Chi to me—he said that I was exactly like Lisa and that my dog was very unhappy and would probably die. I felt like slugging him. He then looked very closely at the white lounging suit I was wearing.

"You must never wear black or red or orange or white because people will not love you."

I'd had enough of his nonsense. "Well, you've got that half right," I snapped. "I'm wearing white right now and I certainly am not enamoured with you! If it's all the same to you, I'd like to send-a-psychic right out my front door!"

And with that last admittedly rude comment of mine, he left.

I received a lot of supportive fan mail during this period from viewers who had obviously read about my divorce in magazines or newspaper columns. I've always considered myself lucky to have attracted such a strong following doing *World* for so many years. Knowing that strangers care about you when you're feeling down and out certainly boosts the old morale.

Of course, not everyone has loved me through the years. Many viewers have gone out of their way to express their displeasure with Lisa, but hate mail is better than no mail: Indifference is the worst possible thing on a soap—it usually leads to contract cancellations! I'm always grateful I've been able to provoke the viewers into feeling something—even if it's hostility.

When I first started doing *World,* my daddy received a letter from a woman in his church which said, "How can you hold your head up in front of your congregation with such a horrible daughter—who did what I saw her do in the bushes with Bruce?" As my early popularity grew, so did the intensity of the reactions of some of the viewers. Television had never offered up a vixen before, and not everyone was enamored by the idea. I once received a dead fish with a note attached that read, "You stink like dead fish!"

I remember the first time I went home to visit my parents after I had made it big on television. The day I arrived, I found dozens and dozens of women crowded around the house, standing out in the yard, looking at me expectantly. I thought they were members of Daddy's congregation. Or perhaps Mother was having a luncheon or a ladies' meeting of some sort. As soon as I strolled up the walk, they all started flocking around me.

"Lisa, it's so good to see you."

"You're even lovelier in person than you are on television."

"I can remember when you sang in the choir!"

I was very flattered and my peacock feathers were beginning to show. There's something very satisfying, if only momentarily, about returning to a place where you once felt rejected or misunderstood and finding out everyone now loves you. If you're the type of person who marches to the beat of a different drummer, like me, it often takes the rest of the world a long time to catch up to you.

I was caught up with the ladies' enthusiasm and invited them into the house. When I walked into the living room, I realized no one was home. I couldn't figure that out. I was still certain the women had been invited by either my mother or father.

They jammed the house, all talking to me at once. They wanted to know about Bob and Chris and Nancy. When Daddy walked in, he thought they were friends of mine, so he went to the kitchen to make coffee for everyone.

Mother was teaching school. When she walked in and saw the house bulging with women, she nearly fainted. She couldn't even get close enough to kiss me, so she ran upstairs to change into something more comfortable until the crowd thinned.

The telephone rang. It was my agent from New York notifying me that I had a very important audition and would have to return immediately. Daddy's expression was forlorn because he had gathered from my conversation that I was leaving.

"I guess this is a hello and a good-bye. I'd better see Mother."

I started moving through the crowd toward the stairs and Mother was standing at the top, wearing a robe and looking terribly distraught. I told her I had to turn right around and fly back.

She shouted above the jabbering, "You will just have to excuse my daughter, please, I haven't even had a chance to see her and now she's leaving us."

She wanted them to go, and she grabbed my hand and started to march me up the stairs.

"Aren't these people friends of yours," she asked.

"No," I replied. "I thought you invited them here."

"Don't be silly, Sweetie."

Daddy came over and said, "I don't know who they are, either."

He asked them politely to please leave. It was then we realized that they had read about my homecoming in the local newspapers. They were my fans!

Once when I was having a romantic dinner with Danny in an Italian restaurant, a fan was able to release her frustrations in a manner that I could only dream of. I had a story line at the time where Lisa was very ill and confined to her bed. Danny and I were in the middle of our first course. A fan approached my table looking like a Sunday school teacher who was about to reprimand her class for talking during church. She circled our table a few times—I thought she was trying to work up the nerve to say hello—and then lurched forward, eyes popping out of her head.

"You scheming bitch!" she blurted out. "I knew it. I just knew it. I kept telling my daughter you weren't really sick. You're fine. And dining with this stranger! Poor Grant Cole-

Danny and I at the beginning of our marriage—very happy and very in love.

Modeling my collection of loungewear for the "Eileen Fulton: At Home" collection.

I was a blonde bombshell for my opening at the Persian Room at The Plaza.

Cuddling my beautiful babies, Sarah and Lala. (*Courtesy of Ira Berger*)

One of my longtime loyal fans, Father Bryer.

Here I am about to go galloping off into the sunset with my cowboy. (*Courtesy of Touch of Crystal*)

My favorite couturier, Miss Frankie, and columnist Anita Summer, at my party at La Folie where I announced I was leaving *ATWT*.

Danny Fortunato, husband No. 2, with his cigar, his tux and his "wife"— Eileen Fulton in her ever present tiara, in that order. (*Courtesy of Day*)

Gregg Mary played my son Tom and was one of my absolute favorites. (*Courtesy of Deborah K. O'Brien*)

I was absolutely ecstatic when I learned Farley Granger was joining the cast of *ATWT*.

This photo was snapped when I still thought I was speaking to the Ambassador of Israel.

When I began receiving death threats, I was escorted in and out of the studio by a policeman.
(*Courtesy of UPI*)

I presented Richard Thomas—who once played my soap son, Tom—with a delicious chocolate birthday cake.

Our birthday cake for the twenty-fifth anniversary of *ATWT*. Pictured left to right are: Billy Johnstone, me, Don McLaughlin, Helen Wagner, and Don Hastings.

I became part owner of The New York Stars—an all women's basketball team.

I was asked to be the Grande Parade Marshall in Charlotte, North Carolina. Danny, on my right, with one of his customary cigars.

Doing charity work and fund-
raising for Unicef and
The March of Dimes.

All dressed up and ready to kill
as the wicked Kaye in *Night Club
Confidential*.

Here I am with one of my favorite actors, Nick Coster. Nick is an ex-husband and current lover—on the show of course!

Kenneth, my fabulous assistant, and I in Greensboro for a concert.

Backstage before one of my nightclub apearances. (*Courtesy of Aubrey Reuben*)

Celebrating my thirty-fifth year on *ATWT.*

man! You should be ashamed of yourselves!"

To emphasize her irritation, she picked up the Ceasar salad I was eating and dumped it on Danny's head. I feigned anguish for my unjustly attacked husband, but inside I wanted to hug the woman and thank her.

Autograph seekers are a particularly overzealous group. A few years ago, I was attending a luncheon at Sardi's when I was pursued by an overly excited fan in the most unusual manner. A bus was parked in front of the restaurant, waiting to transport a large theater party that had come to town for a matinee performance. I stepped into the ladies' room. After a few minutes I could hear several women whispering, "Lisa's in the bathroom—third stall on the left. Pass it on." A heavily perfumed woman with rattling jewelry began crawling under my stall. She smiled at me, thrust a paper towel in my direction, and begged, "Lisa, can I please have an autograph? I'm sorry to bother you, but I'm in a hurry. I don't want to miss my bus."

"No!" I replied. "Please. Not now. If you'll wait outside I'll be happy to accommodate you, but I'm not in a position to give you anything at the moment." The over-eager autograph seeker waited and I signed the paper towel from Sardi's for her. I've autographed some very unusual things in my career, including: stomachs, fannies, arms, diapers (clean ones, of course), money, and tongue depressors for all of the doctors I have visited.

Soap opera fans come from all walks of life—even politics. Someone once told me that in 1967, when Barbara Walters was interviewing the once governor of Texas, John Connally and his wife, they both looked at their watches half-way through the question-and-answer session.

"I'm sorry, Miss Walters," the governor said. "But we'll have to stop for a bit. The Mrs. and I have have to see what Lisa's doing."

"Lisa? Who's Lisa?" Ms. Walters asked.

"You know," the Connallys replied in unison, "on the soap."

She apparently went home and told her father the story—he owned a nightclub called The Latin Quarter—and I was booked there for a night! I suppose I should have given her an agent's fee for the recommendation, but I never did!

I'm always amazed at how well longtime fans remember who's who on the show. I received a letter recently because Nick Coster, who used to play my Husband No. 2, John Eldridge, is now playing my love interest Eduardo Grimaldi. A woman wrote to say, "You can't fool me. I've been watching your show for thirty-two years and I know who Nick Coster is. He played your husband Grant Coleman." I thought, *You're warm, but you're not hot.* Grant was played by the handsome James Douglas.

Nicky is one of my all-time favorite actors. He's such fun to work with. I remember when we were doing *Our Private World* together in 1965, he had a beat-up white convertible that had bullet holes in one of the doors. Nicky loved the car—and the bullet holes! One night after a long day at the studio, he offered to drive me home. The top to his convertible didn't work, so he had left it down for months and the interior had grown layers upon layers of New York City grime. When we reached my apartment, I invited him up for a drink. The night before I had just taken the covers off my new white sofa and chairs. While we sat there conversing, I watched Nicky begin covering my new furniture with tiny little black hand prints. I adored him so much, I never said anything at the time. And I still have a few of his prints on one of the chairs!

I used to get letters from fans saying, "I grew up watching you." Then it was my mother grew up watching you or my grandmother. Two years ago I received a birthday card from a fan.

She wrote, "My great-grandmother started my grandmother who got my mom to watch who turned me on and now I sit with my baby daughter and watch your show so in my family there are five generations of Fulton fans!" Now that's a testimonial!

One of my all-time favorite fan stories centers around *World's* first romantic couple, Penny and Jeff, played by Rosmary Prinz and Mark Rydell, the movie director who went on to make *On Golden Pond*. Mark Rydell wanted out of the show so he could go to Hollywood. The writers decided to kill Jeff— quite a radical decision at the time, because Penny and Jeff were loved across America. The day they married, viewers throughout the country had wedding receptions. Women got dressed up and had parties. This was before the Luke and Laura wedding on *General Hospital* created a similar sensation. Penny and Jeff got a truck load of wedding presents, but the producers sent them back.

One of my fans told me that a friend of hers had been watching the day Jeff died, and she was devastated. She began crying hysterically, shocked by the tragedy, when the telephone rang. It was her husband calling to say he would be late for dinner. When he heard his wife's sobs, he asked her what had happened.

"Darling, what's wrong?"

"You won't believe it!" she cried. "It's awful. It's just so awful."

"Tell me," he urged. "What's the matter."

"It's Jeff. Oh, my God, I can't bear to say it," she sputtered between sobs.

"What—what about Jeff. What happened to him?" It seems the couple had a fourteen-year-old son named Jeff.

"Jeff is dead!" she wailed and once again began crying uncontrollably.

"Oh, my God!" he screamed. "Don't worry. I'll be right

there." He threw down the phone and explained to his boss that he had to leave immediately—his son was dead. Of course, everyone in the office was just sick about the news. The husband darted through mid-day traffic and raced into the house only to discover his wife ironing a shirt.

"Hi, honey," she said quite cheerfully. "What are you doing home so early?"

He thought she had lost her mind with grief. "Tell me. What happened to Jeff?"

"Oh, he was killed in a car crash," she said while spraying some starch on a shirt collar. "Pork chops all right for dinner?"

"What do you mean?" he cried. "What car crash?"

"Well he was with Penny and there was a—"

"Who's Penny?"

"You know. Penny. They were married."

The husband thought his wife had completely lost her mind. "What in the world are you talking about!?" he finally screamed.

"On the soap. They killed Jeff on the soap today."

Apparently the next time he was going to be late for dinner, he had his secretary telephone.

A priest named Father Briar was one of my most devoted, longtime fans who eventually became a good friend. He had gotten hooked on watching *World* when he was in an automobile accident and was convalescing. He started to write to me and joined my fan club. One year we held a contest: Whoever could bring in the most new members would be awarded a beautiful pink straw hat I had worn on the show. Father Briar enticed half of his congregation to join my fan club and won the prize. Melissa, who ran the club, sent him a letter: "Dear Father Briar, Congratulations! You have certainly won the pink straw hat. Since, however, you probably don't have any use for the hat, we would love to send you some photographs and mementos of Eileen's from the show." Father Briar wrote back to us and said he'd love to have the mementos, but most of all he wanted the straw hat. "After all," he wrote, "if the Pope can wear a red hat, surely I can own a pink one." When I read his letter, I realized what a delightful sense of humor he had.

Father Briar traveled around the country to many of my nightclub openings. He was there my first night at the Persian Room, he consoled me when a relative was ill, and he certainly lent an ear during my breakup with Danny. Father Briar always sent me beautiful flowers and thoughtful gifts for holidays and birthdays. He especially loved butterflies as they represented rebirth. He died a few years ago, but I have many lovely keepsakes that remind me of him.

Not all my experiences with fans have been so lighthearted. A woman once approached me after an autograph-signing session and related a story that makes me cry even today. I was doing a personal appearance in a department store and had signed what I hoped was the last autograph for the day. But then I turned around and saw a woman dressed in a navy blue suit, staring at me with the saddest expression on her face.

"Can I help you?" I asked. She didn't respond. "Are you all right?"

She continued to stare into my eyes, searching, probing, trying to figure something out. Finally she spoke in a whisper.

"Why is it that when my mother died she asked for you?"

"What are you talking about?" I asked softly.

"You were the last person on my mother's lips. I need to know why."

"I'm sorry," I said. "I still don't understand what you're talking about."

"My mother was hospitalized. She was dying. Our entire family was gathered around her with the minister. She had been watching your soap every day in the hospital, wondering whether you would survive your bout of pneumonia. And then she slipped into a coma. When she came to, I took her hand and looked into her eyes. All she said was 'Is Lisa going to be all right?' I didn't know what she was talking about at first, but then I remembered that you were Mama's soap person. So the minister told her, 'Yes, don't worry. Lisa's going to be fine.' 'I'm so glad,' Mama answered. And then she died.''

The woman lost control and began sobbing. I tried to comfort her, but she was obviously angry with me.

"Why! Why did my mother have to die with your name on her lips?"

I let her catch her breath for a minute. "I don't know exactly," I began, "but I have an idea. I was with her every day. I distracted her from her troubles. I was just helping you take care of your mother. That's what soaps do. They're there to provide a familiar face or to be a friend who'll visit you when no one else can. We're just there to make people feel like they're not alone in the world."

My words seemed to comfort her. She thanked me and walked away. I meant what I said. I realize acting on a soap isn't like performing brain surgery—some people think it's just a lot of nonsense about nothing. But I'm proud of what I do, if for no other reason than for the fact that an elderly woman or a young college student can feel a little less alone for a half hour or an hour each day. They can feel excited or hopeful for the characters, or even disappointed and sad. But at least they're feeling something.

They say that "when it rains it pours." Those first two years after I left Danny, I got drenched. Nothing went right. First, I caught a viral infection and had to take a six-week leave of absence from the show. They replaced me with Betsy Von Furstonberg because Lisa's story line was so heavy at the time. It was frustrating lying in a hospital bed watching Betsy in my dress and my ballgown, playing scenes that I wanted to play. I ended up returning before I was ready and collapsed on the set.

While I was recuperating, Patsy Anne Pepper introduced me to a cute and cuddly multimillionaire friend named Dexter. He began a proper courtship, taking me to romantic restaurants like Sign of the Dove and the Rainbow Room. When my divorce became final, Patsy, Dexter, and I went out on the town to celebrate. For a short time, Dexter and I had a fabulous affair, but then I began to think he was a pathological liar. Dexter would make a date and then telephone me at half-hour intervals from different locations in the city, apologizing for his delays with the most unbelievable excuses.

"Darling, I'm sorry I'm late, but my car just had a flat tire and I don't have a spare."

"I hate to keep you waiting, darling, but I'm in the middle of a meeting that could net me a million."

"Now, don't worry, but I'm rushing to the hospital. I have a horrible pain in my side—could be appendicitis."

And that was all in *one* night!

After we'd been dating for about two months, Dexter suggested we go on a hot-air balloon ride. I had recently read an article describing a particular inn in upstate New York that organized weekend balloon trips: They took you up in the morning and met you with a champagne picnic lunch when the balloon landed. After a few hours of rest, they would take you up in the evening and then meet you with a candlelight dinner. All for $1,000. It sounded wonderfully romantic. I discussed it with Dexter and we agreed to go. Dexter asked if I would take care of the $500 deposit because he was so busy. He assured me I would be reimbursed.

A few hours before our trip, Dexter telephoned to cancel,

assuring me that I would get the lost deposit back.

"I'm so sorry, darling, but I'm just dead on my feet from working so hard on my computer thing. I think I'm coming down with pneumonia or something. I've got to stay in bed for at least a couple of days."

"You poor thing," I said. "Don't worry about it. You just rest and get yourself well." Of course, by then, I was beginning to have suspicions, but I pushed them away. The poor darling sounded so awful.

A month later I was having lunch with some friends. One of the women mentioned the upstate balloon trip.

"You know, Eileen. I almost forgot. My husband and I went on that fabulous balloon excursion and the owners said that Eileen Fulton and her boyfriend had been there a few weeks earlier and had a wonderful time. Didn't you just love it!"

"Wait a minute," I snapped. "They said *I* was there?"

"Yes," she replied. "In fact they mentioned you even gave them an autograph."

I couldn't believe it! Dexter went with some other woman pretending to be me on my $500 deposit. I quickly put an end to that affair.

I was getting soaked, but I wasn't out of the storm yet. In the midst of this emotional chaos, I discovered that my dear, sweet press agent, Patsy Anne, was overbilling me. Being raised a preacher's daughter, I tend to be the trusting type. I give people the benefit of the doubt until they prove me wrong. I was becoming suspicious of Patsy Anne's bills, because they seemed to be getting higher and higher. One day I went to the Polo Lounge—one of my hideouts at the time—with all of my bills and a calculator. I parked myself in a booth and went through everything. It didn't take an accountant to figure out that she had been overcharging me. I was paying for Patsy's entire phone bill, a home care attendant for her mother, all of her meals and cab rides in the city, and the rental fees on all her office equipment. I met with Patsy in my apartment, presented my findings, and promptly fired her on the spot. When I fell into bed that night, I remember thinking, *Enough, enough! When are the clouds going to break?*

My glimmer of sunlight occurred as Doug Marland began to reshape and revitalize the show. Doug had made quite a name for himself in the soap industry writing for *General Hospital* and *Guiding Light*. But I remembered him as the young actor who played the small part of a doctor on our show when Lisa was in the midst of her "phantom fetus" story line. I hated that story line more than any I've ever played. I had to wander around for months saying, "I'm pregnant and I don't know how. I've never been this pregnant before." That seemed so foolish. I had already had four husbands and two children. Surely I must have known how it happened.

A few weeks into the story line, I received a letter from a woman in Birmingham, Alabama. She enclosed a pamphlet from Planned Parenthood with a note attached that read, *"This is how it happened—now get on with it!"* The producers finally decided enough was enough. It was time to reveal everything. Suddenly Lisa was rushed into the hospital. Her doctor, played by the young Doug Marland, accompanied her into the operating room. The entire three-month story line had built up to this moment. As the doctor prepared to do a C-section to save the baby, he looked down and said, "There's nothing there!" The shocker of all shockers! Nobody knew it was a phantom fetus—not even Lisa—until the final moment of the show.

Doug was embarrassed at having to say the line. He thought the whole plot was ridiculous.

"I think we're in trouble with this one," he said at the time. "We need a writer. I'll have to help this show and write something for the scene." It's ironic considering he went on to become one of the best writers in the business. The director picked on Doug at the time, but I tried to calm him, saying, "You're just new. The director likes to have a little fun with all the new actors. Don't worry. You'll be fine." I know he was grateful and appreciated my words of encouragement.

Doug revitalized Lisa for me. I hadn't been that excited about story lines and scenes since the days of Irna. He used to telephone and say, "I have this great idea. What would you think if . . ." Having been an actor first, Doug made every effort to allow *World*'s actors to have as much input as possible in what was happening to their characters. Everyone appreciated his efforts.

A few years after he arrived, I presented Doug with an idea that turned out to be one of my favorite, albeit brief, story lines about menopause. Irna had attempted to deal with the subject once, but it didn't go over well. She created a scenario about a woman who had to have a hysterectomy, hiring a wonderful actress to play the part. But the audience just didn't care. They wanted to get back to the characters they knew. That's when Irna realized you don't bring in new characters to deal with certain subjects. You give the story lines to characters the viewers already know. That's why so many horrible problems happen to a single character on a soap.

I had approached Doug when I began to experience some medical problems and was diagnosed as being premenopausal. I felt reaching that particular stage in life was nothing to be ashamed of—every woman has to go through it. I used to tease the younger actresses by saying, "Don't be hasty. It's nothing to be ashamed of. Hot flashes are just wonderful because the cute guys at the cold studio love to get close to a radiating stove." Doug thought it was a wonderful idea. I even went on Dr. Ruth's show to discuss the story line and the topic.

Doug wrote a moving scene in which Lisa is jealous of Kim, her former husband Bob's new wife, because Kim has just had a baby. Lisa holds the newborn, loving it at first. Then remembering that she can never have a baby again, she begins to hate what the child represents. Lisa has a hot flash, thrusts the infant into its mother's arms, and runs outside, where she picks a fight with Bob and falls apart. It was a fabulous scene and I got a lot of mail from women who could relate to that moment.

It's wonderful working with a writer who is approachable, because it lessens the odds for those unpleasant "on-the-set-showdowns" when an actor refuses to say a particular line as written or do a particular piece of business. Other than the time I wanted to say the word *pregnant,* there was only one occasion in which I created a fuss and refused to play a scene. Lisa was planning a surprise party for one of her husbands, reuniting him with his children. The husband found out about the party and the joke was on Lisa. The way the scene was written, I was supposed to serve him a slice of birthday cake. He was then to tell me that he knew about the surprise. Not believing him, Lisa and he were to have a little spat and she was to throw the cake in his face. He was then supposed to pick me up and spank me in front of the guests.

"I won't do it!" I argued vehemently in rehearsal. "I won't allow it!"

"You have to," the producer retorted. "That's the end of the show."

You never fooled with the end of the show. It was like something written in stone by the hand of God. And it also affected the beginning of the next day's work, because you usually started with the scene you last played. I knew it was a serious thing to make them alter this last moment, but I was adamant.

"I'm sorry," I continued, "but I will not have him spank me. I don't think it's cute when a man spanks a woman. I think it's violent and macho and horrible and abusive and I will not do it."

I was revved up to deliver one of those speeches about the

role of women like Julia Sugerbaker on *Designing Women.* "If you insist, I'll get in touch with NOW and we'll march on you."

We were definitely at an impasse.

Fortunately, one of the assistant producers had an idea. "What if after you hit him with the cake he smiles, gives you a big kiss, gets the frosting all over your face, and everyone laughs?"

I considered the idea for a moment. "Sure. I'll buy that. Just as long as he doesn't smack me because if he does I, Eileen Fulton, will kick the livin' daylights out of him. Lisa would stab him with the cake knife, but I'm too ladylike to use a knife!"

Everyone was pleased with the speedy resolution. We were lucky. Those kinds of disputes don't always work out so amicably.

After my affair with the pathological computer millionaire, I decided to try something a little different. I went out with a hunk of a man named Larry Paladino, a real cowboy who lived in my building. He was fabulous! I was singing "Ki-yi-yippy-yippy-yay" for days. Larry used to say, "Little lady, you've got to have somebody to take care of you and get rid of these bad people in your life. And I'd just love to help you." He was very cute.

Larry got mad at me one night and yelled, "I'm sick and tired of the way you act. You've got to let me take care of you because I love you, Goddamn it!" Then he marched out the front door, slamming it behind him. I thought it was a funny way to declare one's love. He was fun, but I knew I wasn't ready to settle down and sing "Home on the Range."

By the beginning of 1983, I was beginning to feel like I was in a rut: I wanted more time off from my hectic schedule at *World* to

pursue such outside interests as singing and theater. My contrac-
tual agreement gave me some time off, but I wanted more. I had
just completed a popular story line so the producers were not
very enthusiastic about giving me more "off screen" time. I
think they're always afraid that if you disappear for too long, the
audience will either forget about you or lose interest.

I've never found that to be true. If the audience likes your
character and you've been on long enough for them to get to
know you, they'll always be ready for you when you return. In
the world of soaps, "out of sight" is not necessarily "out of
mind."

I didn't know it at the time, but my contract renewal was
about to become one of the great public debates of 1983.

# NINE

# Kill Lisa? Over My Dead Body!

A month before my contract was up for renewal, I was in the executive producer's office at the end of a long day. We were both tired, but I needed to discuss my schedule for the coming week. While we coordinated the dates and times, Ms. Executive Producer—who was certainly not at the top of anyone's popularity list—sipped a glass of wine and rocked back and forth in her chair.

"You know, Eileen," she began as if she were thinking aloud to herself. "I have the best plan. You realize this is the time of youth, don't you."

It was a rhetorical question, but I felt obligated to respond. "Yes," I said.

"Well, I've finally figured out a way to get rid of all the old contract players, you know, the old-timers. I think they're just dragging the show down."

I couldn't believe she was saying this to *me*. Didn't she realize *I* was one of the "old-timers," as she put it. I'd been on *World* for twenty-three years. And although I recognized the importance of the "kids," as I called them, I didn't think it had to be at the expense of such old favorites as Don or Helen or me. I was dying to find out what the producer was planning, so I played along.

"Really. You're going to get rid of them. How on earth will you manage that?"

"It's so simple," she chuckled, and continued to rock in her chair. The producer had a glass desk, so I could see her shoes rise and fall to the rhythm of her speech. "We just write the old ones in less and less, no story line, just less and less, and then, finally, one day, they just disappear. The audience will be so involved in the exciting plots of all the young characters, no one will ever miss them."

I was shocked and couldn't believe what I was hearing. Eliminating the original characters was like removing the foundation of a building. Something was bound to come crashing down. *If you just want to target the youth market, why not create a new show on which all the main characters are kids,* I thought at the time. I felt that to make choices geared for a specific segment of our audience was wrong—and certainly unfair to the older, loyal viewers who had watched us for so many years.

"I think you're dead wrong. Those characters have a loyal following and they'll surely be missed if you try something like that." The producer just laughed and continued to sip her wine.

I was haunted by that conversation for days. It definitely had an impact on my decision about leaving the show. After carefully thinking it through, I decided that I needed more than four weeks off a year. I wanted six months on, six months off. I felt like I was stagnating and didn't like the story line at the time. Lisa had just married Whit McColl and it wasn't going anywhere. I was known for playing the conniving, scheming, lying bitch. That's what the viewers wanted to see me play. But Lisa was losing her punch. I watched Joan Collins in an episode of *Dynasty* and wondered why I wasn't doing *that.* In the midst of my decision-making process, I received a phone call from an old classmate.

"Hi, darlin'. This is Stora Boone."

"Who?" I couldn't remember anyone called Stora.

"Stora Boone. You'll remember me as Frank Boone from The Neighborhood Playhouse. Everyone calls me Stora now."

Finally it clicked. Adorable Frank. Curly hair, dimples, and knobby knees! Frank and I had, indeed, been classmates together, but I couldn't count back that many years and I hadn't spoken to him since. "My goodness, Frank. How are you?"

"I'm just fine, darlin'. I've got this wonderful dinner theater down in New Orleans and I'd just love for you to come down and do *Goodbye Charlie*. It's just a bit of fluff but funny as hell. And if you don't want to do that, we'll produce whatever you say. You just tell us!" I'd never known a producer to be so accommodating. Because I wasn't sure what my availability would be, I said I'd get back to him in a week or two. His offer got me thinking. I telephoned Tom Korman, my agent in Los Angeles, and told him to line up as much theater as he could for the coming year. If my upcoming negotiations with *World* didn't work out, at least I would have a place to work.

My manager, Pete, flew in from Los Angeles to handle the negotiations. We had lunch before we met with the executive producer and I told him exactly where I stood.

"Pete, I'm prepared to walk if I don't get the time off. I'm not worried. I've got dinner theaters lined up, so it's not like I'll be sitting at home waiting for the phone to ring."

We went to our meeting with Ms. Executive Producer. She appeared to remain quite calm as I listed my demands. But then I noticed her heels were rising off the floor—I could see them through her glass desk. By the time I had finished speaking, her feet were sticking straight out, as if she were resting them on a footstool. She obviously wasn't as relaxed as she appeared to be. After approximately fifteen minutes, she concluded the meeting by stating that it was highly unlikely my demands would be met, but she would get back to me as soon as possible.

The tabloid press had a wonderful time chronicling my

negotiations, with such playful headlines in the *New York Post* as
"The Bitch Gets Out Her Claws: Will She Quit or Won't She?"
Four days before my contract was up, I appeared on *Good Morning America*. The interviewer asked if I would really leave the
show or if this was just a press ploy for more money. Despite
what everyone thinks, it isn't *always* about the money.

"Of course I'll leave," I replied. "I'm not backing down." I
asked them to pan in for a close-up. I looked straight into the
camera and made an announcement to my producers:

"I hope you're watching. You've got four days left—count
'em, one-two-three-four—to give me what I want or I'm out of
here! I'm history! I'm going to California!"

*GMA* loved it—it was great television—but the producers
were horrified when I went to the studio later that morning.
One of the cast members took great exception to my behavior:

"Really, Eileen," she stated, "most of us do not appreciate
your negotiating your contract on the air. It's not very dignified."

"Well, darling, if you can do better, please be my guest—or
my agent!"

The last couple of days were tense. With the assistance of my
new, talented, and adorable press agent, David Granoff, a huge
party at La Folie was planned for the night before my last day.
Everyone was invited—including all the media—and they were
told I would announce my final decision during the festivities.
*Entertainment Tonight* was going to tape the event, but they
stayed away at the last minute, convinced it was just a huge
publicity stunt. Almost everyone said, "Of course she's going
back to the show. It's her bread and butter. She's just maneuvering for more money."

My family attended the party along with Phyllis Diller, Virginia Graham, and Joan Bennett. I wore a drop-dead powder
blue sequined dress with dolman sleeves, very short to the

knee—it was definitely a show stopper as Miss Frankie had promised. And my hair was also very short at the time and dyed fire red. At the designated hour, I walked up to the microphone. After thanking everyone for attending, I announced that I was *not* going back to *World*.

"Tomorrow is my last day as Lisa!"

Everyone was in shock. The crowd went wild as reporters began firing questions. The photographers couldn't change film fast enough. I told the crowd that I had contracts with dinner theaters lined up for a year.

"Don't you worry about me. I'll be just fine!"

And then I left.

I enjoyed most of the following year traveling around the country performing in dinner theaters—back in the days when "star" dinner theaters were popular. Zsa Zsa Gabor was on the circuit, along with Imogine Coca, Syd Charisse, Robert Reed, and other actors who had done television. It was invigorating performing in front of a live audience again. My fans were overjoyed by the chance to see Lisa "live."

My first stop was Stora Boone's theater in New Orleans, where I performed the lead in *Goodbye Charlie*. Stora couldn't have been kinder or more accommodating. He housed me in a lovely suite at a beautiful hotel and insisted I bring my two dogs, Sarah and Lala. He even paid for my secretary-assistant to accompany me. The show was tremendously successful and we extended the run for two more weeks.

On closing night, Stora organized a wild and wonderful party at his home. He hired a woman to do an elaborate ice sculpture of a swan. Waiters served lavish hors d'oeuvres around the periphery of the pool. Half way through the party, one of the guests decided that the swan would be much happier in the water. He tossed the sculpture into the pool—no easy feat considering its size and weight! Unfortunately, the woman who created the sculpture was also at the party. She took one look at her labor of love as it began sinking to the bottom and jumped in to save the drowning bird. I can still see this middle-aged lady in a brown suit and sensible pumps splashing her way to the rescue. I was feeling a bit tipsy that night, so I didn't wait to see if she was able to save it.

I next traveled to Canada to do Neil Simon's *Plaza Suite*. I loved that particular show because it consisted of three one-act plays. It provided me with an opportunity to create three very different women. For the character in the first act, I had a padded suit made so I would look like a more mature woman with a middled-aged spread. I did my hair and makeup to look puffy, dowdy, and a bit wrinkled. I admit I looked different, but I didn't look awful. When I came out on stage for my first appearance, the audience was absolutely silent. And then I could hear a few people whisper, "Is that her? Naw, that's not her. Wait a minute, there's only two people in this show—it's got to be her!" Then the gasps would begin, followed by, "What a shame she let herself go. Look how fat she got. Poor girl, must be so miserable not being on television she just went and ate herself silly." I waddled around in my fat suit for the entire first act to the sympathy of the audience.

Of course I couldn't wait for the second act to begin: I played Muriel, a feisty, feminine female in a form-fitting dress. The moment my svelte frame burst through the door, the audience went wild with laughter and applause. They must have thought I went on a crash diet and lost forty pounds during the intermission so as not to disappoint them!

Working in the theater on a regular basis made me feel like I was back on *World* during the days of live television. It was so exciting because you just never knew what might go wrong. When I was in Canton, Ohio, performing in *It Had to Be You* with Ray Stewart, I hurt myself during the first act. We were in the middle of a fight scene, and I was supposed to rush and tackle Ray to keep him from leaving. As I pivoted, my foot caught on the rug and suddenly I felt something rip in my leg. I couldn't move. I thought I might have burst a blood vessel. While I grew faint, I began to picture the headlines: "Actress Dies on Stage" and "Break a Leg, Not a Blood Vessel."

Instead of physically stopping Ray, as scripted, I said, "If you walk out that door, I'm going to faint." Ray just looked at me like "Where did that line come from?"

"You're going to *what?*" he asked.

"Faint. Faint. F–A–I–N–T. I'm going to faint dead away and then what will you do." I was trying to stay alive and keep the scene going until I could figure out what to do. My days in live television had trained me well: *Keep playing no matter what!*

Ray walked up to me and whispered, "Are you all right?"

I wasn't ready to give up the scene. Maintaining my character, I said, "No, I'm not all right! In fact I think I'm going to DIE!" The next thing I knew, Ray was carrying me to the bed on the set. I was getting dizzier by the second and the audience was screaming with laughter because they thought it was all part of the scene. After carefully placing me on the bed, Ray walked directly downstage and uttered that classic line: "Is there a doctor in the house?"

The audience went wild, stomping their feet, screaming with laughter.

"No, I'm serious," he urged.

They began applauding.

"He means it," I gasped. "I'm not well."

They all rose to their feet.

For a second I thought, *Well, if I've got to die on stage at least it's going to be to a standing ovation.* Finally the stage manager walked out and calmed the audience, explaining the circumstances. He said that there would be a brief intermission until he could determine whether I would be able to continue.

"Now don't go away. I'll be right back," I yelled as they carried me off stage to another huge round of applause. I knew that I wouldn't get paid unless I completed the first act. Ever the business-minded actress I was determined to at least try.

The Emergency Medical Service arrived and began prodding, poking, and asking questions.

"We can't be certain what it is until we run some tests," said one of the technicians. "How old are you."

It was a week before my birthday. "I'm forty-nine."

"Oh, God, really?! That old?"

I didn't know whether to be insulted that they thought forty-nine was old or flattered that they didn't think I looked my age.

"It could be a heart attack."

"What do you mean, it's in my leg!" I screamed.

"Well either way, you can't go back on stage."

"I have to finish this act. At least let me try."

I grabbed a plunger and hobbled back on stage to finish, and the audience loved it. When the curtain came down I apologized:

"I'm sorry to have to cut this short, but I really have to go to the hospital now. Thanks for being so understanding. Come see us again."

The EMS workers whisked me to the emergency room of a nearby hospital, where they started running all kinds of tests. There I was, trapped in a bed in the ER, when I suddenly realized I had to go to the bathroom, but they wouldn't let me out of the bed.

"I'm sorry, but you can't move until we find out what's wrong with you. If it's a heart attack, you could do yourself some serious damage."

*What is this obsession with heart attacks,* I thought. *Just because of my age?* One of the nurses brought me one of those nasty little stainless steel bedpans and pulled a curtain around me. I looked at my reflection in the bottom of the dish and got very depressed. Just as I was trying to decide if I could hold on a while longer, the curtains parted. A crowd of nurses and doctors surrounded me—and they all wanted an *autograph!*

"Go away. Can't you see I need some privacy?"

"We don't mind," one of the nurses replied, thrusting a pen in my face. "We're used to this."

"Well, I'm not!" I yelled, yanking the curtain back around me. After all the tests were in, they told me I had ripped a muscle. The next day, I was back on stage with a crutch, doing what I love best.

A few months later, while I was performing in Tampa, my father had a heart attack. I was desperate to get home to him, but with only one day off it wasn't easy. My last show was on a Sunday night. As soon as it ended, I got on a late plane and flew to Asheville and then took a cab to my parents' house. Daddy was in ICU at the hospital. The moment I walked into his room and saw his face light up, I breathed a sigh of relief. At least he could recognize his "old girl." I sat by his bedside for hours, just studying his face, remembering all the words of encouragement he had given me through the years. I prayed harder than I had ever in my life, hoping he would recover.

Forty-eight hours later, I was back on stage in front of an audience, trying to entertain hundreds of people who had driven for miles to see their favorite femme fatal. I stayed in daily contact with my mother, and she assured me Daddy's condition was improving. After I finished my two-week run in Tampa, I flew to the Midwest to do a silly show called *Squabbles.* While I was there, I decided it was stupid to be running around the country trying to make people laugh when my daddy was so sick. I decided to alter my schedule. After one more week of performances, I would take several weeks off and help my mother nurse Daddy back to health.

That following Friday afternoon, two days before my last show, I decided to take a nap before the evening performance. I was exhausted because I had spent many sleepless nights worrying about my father. About 5 P.M. the telephone rang, waking me from my nap. It was my mother.

"Hello, Sweetie," she said quietly and then paused for what seemed like an eternity. I knew what she was about to say. In the span of no more than a few seconds, my mind flashed through what seemed like hundreds of photographs of my father at different stages in my life. When she finally whispered, "Daddy slipped away," the photo album slammed shut and I thought, *Dear God, just let me get hold of myself.*

After briefly speaking with my mother, I telephoned the theater—it was now 5:30 P.M. and we were sold out for that evening's performance. When I told the producer what had happened, he was very kind and understanding. He offered to cancel the show. I thought about it for a minute, but, remembering a conversation I had had with a fan just a week before, I told him I would go on.

Exactly one week earlier, I was signing autographs after the performance and a very tall woman with white hair approached me. She was wearing a chain with a railroad watch attached, which made me think of Daddy—he loved trains. I complimented her on the watch, and she said it was her husband's. She told me he had been with the railroad and had passed away a few days earlier. She went on to explain that she had come to the theater that night because her family thought it might be good for her. Extending two very delicate hands, she said, "You have made me laugh again and given me a reason to go on. Thank you so much for helping me. I wouldn't have missed it for the world." I was obviously very touched by her kind words.

I kept picturing this wonderful woman and her husband's railroad watch when the producer said we could cancel. I thought if there are others like that in the audience tonight, I can't let them down. My not performing wouldn't bring my daddy back, and there wasn't a plane for North Carolina that night in any case—so I decided to perform.

I sat in my dressing room minutes before the performance, staring in the mirror, trying to pull myself together. As I gazed into the eyes of the woman before me, I caught a glimpse of my daddy—of a man who had both a passion for life and compassion for his fellow man. I winked at the man in the mirror.

"This one's for you, Daddy, because you've made me laugh and made me feel so alive."

I walked out on that stage and it was magnetic.

After attending my father's funeral, I spent a week with my mother, talking, mourning, and remembering. I decided I needed a rest, and New York was not the place for peace and quiet, so I headed out West. Stora helped me locate a lovely house in Studio City near Taluca Lake in California, so I got all of my furniture and belongings out of storage in New York and had everything shipped to Los Angeles. I filled my days relaxing in my new house in the hills, visiting with friends, and thinking a lot about Daddy. Putting my professional life on hold, I began making the social rounds of Los Angeles dinner parties with Ross Hunter and Jacques Mapes. And since I was now a resident of the "city of merging freeways," I decided it might be a good time to learn how to drive and get a license.

The guy who taught me was a preacher's son. Based on my background, I should've known he would be trouble. His strict upbringing certainly influenced his approach to driving. The instructor loved to take me for practice drives on Sunset Boulevard at 5 P.M. because all of the hookers would be out advertising their wares. These women were not the type to be intimidated by anything. They loved to have fun with the driving students and I was no exception. The minute they saw my car with the "California Driving School" emblem, they headed my way. While these Amazonian women pressed their free-floating flesh against the windshield, my instructor (who was definitely *not* keeping his eyes on the road) began to roar, "Wow, would you look at that!"

"I can't," I cried out. "I'm trying to drive!"

It was really horrible, but he thought it was a hoot.

Pete, my L.A.-based manager, invited me to lunch one day. It was one of those celebrity hangouts on Melrose, the kind of place where even the valets who park your car are six-foot-two hunks who have $20,000 worth of dental work smiling at you. Halfway through lunch, Pete began to complain of a severe headache. I told him I had some Tylenol in my purse, but he refused.

"C'mon, Eileen, this is L.A. Tylenol for a headache? That's just too funny."

He laughed uncontrollably and removed a small plastic case from the inside pocket of his designer suit. When he flipped open the lid, I saw that the container was divided into eight compartments of equal size, each slot holding a particular kind of pill. Pete began lining up his collection of pills like they were a battalion of soldiers preparing for war. I recognized a few— dalmaine, valium, percodan—and wondered which he would select. A chill ran through me as I watched him scoop up his "troops" and make them disappear with a double martini.

"Pete, don't you have to drive through the canyon to your house in Studio City? Don't you think that's a bit much?"

"You're such a hoot," he chuckled. "No, I'll be fine. I don't even feel it."

If that's how he was handling his body, I could only wonder what he was doing with my career.

By the beginning of 1984, I was getting restless, anxious to start working on a new project but not being able to decide what it would be. Television? Theater? My nightclub act? Lying by my pool one morning, reading Lynda Hirsch's soap column in the *Los Angeles Times,* I thought, *Let me find out what's happening on World.* I was surprised to read that Betsy Von Furstonberg, who had replaced me, wasn't getting along with Robert Horton, who played Whit McColl, Lisa's latest husband. According to the column, she was planning to leave the show and get married, and the producers were going to kill Lisa.

Kill Lisa! I was furious. *Over my dead body,* I thought. I had created the character and devoted over two decades of my life to her, so I immediately telephoned the office.

"Is it true? Is it really true? I can't believe you would actually *kill* Lisa!"

"We're seriously thinking about it," the executive producer said.

"That's kind of stupid." I couldn't stand the thought of anyone else breathing Lisa's final words. She was mine—even though I gave her up it wasn't with the intention that someone else was going to throw her away for good.

Before I even had a chance to think, the words were out of my mouth. "Well, then, let me come back and kill her myself. If you're really going to do it, *I* should be the one to play the death scene. People won't believe she's really dead unless they see *me* die. You know it's true." I really went back with the intention of dying. If I hadn't read Lynda's column, who knows if I ever would have found my way back to the show.

One week later, I was in New York, breathing life back into the woman I had created twenty-three years earlier. Lisa was more wacky the third time around—perhaps because Elizabeth Hubbard had taken over as the resident bitch playing Lucinda Walsh, the business woman with a heart of stone. Nevertheless, I was happy to be back among old friends and familiar environments.

The producers decided that for my first scene I would return from a worldwide shopping spree, surrounded by all of my purchases. To get into the part, I went to Miss Frankie and told her to select a fabulous wardrobe for Lisa for the coming year. I spent over $30,000 on clothes I wore only on the show. After two decades, I knew that part of the attraction to Lisa was the way she dressed. Even if I'm leaving my apartment building to run to the corner store, I always make sure I'm "dressed." It's disappointing from a fan's perspective if they perceive you as a glamour queen and you're slumping down the street in a pair of sweat pants and sneakers.

I try not to repeat dresses when I know I'm going to be photographed but sometimes I just plain forget. I remember reading about Nancy Reagan and how she kept track of what she wore with little index cards attached to each dress stating when it was worn and where—but I'm just too scattered to even think about doing that. A lot of the actors will borrow fancy dresses from the show for a special appearance, but I do not use something that has already been seen by millions of viewers. I think it takes some of the fun out it.

Although I had relocated back to New York, I decided to keep my house in Los Angeles. When I initially signed a new contract with *World,* I thought I would explore that fast-paced, fun-filled, exciting life of "bicoastal actors": I would tape the soap a few days in Manhattan and meet and greet Hollywood's directors and casting people the rest of the week. After about a year of logging more frequent-flyer miles than a stack of stewardesses, I decided to concentrate all of my energies on the East Coast. I fired my pill-popping manager, packed up the house in the hills, and moved everything into a lovely house I purchased in Connecticut. It was heartbreaking to give up my L.A. residence, but as I had learned from my daddy, you have to make your home where your work is—a truth that applies to actors as well as preachers.

In a matter of months, I was rewarded for my sacrifice: I got a call out of the blue to do an off-Broadway musical. I couldn't believe my luck! Finally an opportunity to sing and dance as well as act. And the character was a real bitch. I'd finally have a chance to exercise some of those old Lisa characteristics. I was overjoyed!

The only problem: I had less than two weeks to get ready.

# TEN

# Laugh and the Ratings Go Down

*A* few months after I had returned to New York, I started getting terrible headaches. It reached the point where I could barely focus: I had one constant pain gnawing a hole in my head. Some days it was so unbearable I was afraid that it would start showing on my face while I was taping *World*. When I realized the problem was not going to disappear, I went to a doctor. He ran a series of tests, but they all came back negative.

"It might just be tension headaches, Miss Fulton," the doctor said. "I know you work in a difficult environment."

"I've been in stressful situations all my life, and I've never experienced anything like this before."

"It might be triggered by an emotional reaction to a particular set of circumstances."

Right. Anytime a woman has a pain and it can't be easily diagnosed, it *must* be in her heart or her head. I was revved up and ready to deliver a speech, but I decided to invest my energies instead in finding out what was wrong. After spinning through Manhattan's revolving door of specialists, I finally found Dr. Joseph Marbach. He was able to tell me I had atypical facial neuralgia. I've since learned proper diagnosis is absolutely vital when dealing with any illness. If you don't know what's wrong, how can you begin treatment?

The muscle tissue and nerve endings in my face and throughout my body had become inflamed—which is what initially created the pain. My doctor treated the disorder through a series of injections, which relaxed the inflamed muscle. In a matter of weeks the pain subsided somewhat. I was lucky to have found this particular doctor. He began treating me for this illness back in 1984, and I've been seeing him ever since.

Before I was properly diagnosed, however, I began taking pain killers so that I could make it through the day without screaming nonstop—not that loud, irrational behavior would be considered abnormal in a city like Manhattan. One particular afternoon, I rushed home after a difficult day at the studio, popped two pain killers, and tried to rest, but five minutes later the phone rang. The producers from the off-Broadway hit, *Nightclub Confidential,* were insisting that I come see their show that evening.

"I can't. I just got home and my head is splitting."

"Eileen, you'll be sorry if you don't. I know you'll love the show, and you're perfect for the part, but we have to move quickly. P-l-e-a-s-e!"

The sound of producers pleading does not soothe the savage beast—and it does even less to deaden the temple-torturing pain of a severe headache. I decided to quickly cut my losses. "All right, fine, I'll be there. But I'm not going to guarantee that I'll be a laugh a minute."

"Don't worry. All you have to do is show up and look fabulous. We'll do the rest."

I took a quick look in the mirror and wondered if I was up to the challenge. Perhaps a little diversion might take my mind off my "mind." I quickly telephoned a friend who agreed to accompany me. Although I was feeling a little disoriented from the pills, I managed to transform myself into a glamorous diva.

I fell in love with the show the moment it began. The score was full of that fabulous music from the forties and fifties, like "That Old Black Magic." The producers wanted me to replace the lead and play Kay, a once-famous nightclub singer who was making a comeback. She was sexy, bitchy, funny, and fun. The original lead had broken her ankle. The producers felt that the understudy—who I saw that evening and who was fabulous—didn't have a big enough name to draw a crowd. The moment the applause died down and the house lights came up, the producers rushed over.

"Well, did we lie or what!"

"I loved it. Yes, yes, I'll do it. I can't wait."

"Great, because you have less than two weeks to learn eleven songs, the dance routines, and the lines. But to someone who's done live television and is used to learning a new script every day, I'm sure it'll be a snap!"

"Only two weeks?" I gasped.

"Less."

"Well, then, let's get started!"

The next day I began working with the musical director. Between puffs of a menthol cigarette, he kept assuring me I would be fine. He chain-smoked all day and night, which worked wonders on my vocal chords. If the rehearsal hall wasn't smoky, you knew he'd left for the day. The choreographer began taking me through the paces of the syncopated dance routines. For a woman in her fifties who hadn't been "hoofin-it-up" of late, I managed to hold my own. After a few days, I relaxed enough to enjoy the physicality of the work.

My opening night for *Nightclub Confidential* was the only time in my professional life that I was literally terrified to perform. David Granoff, my fabulous publicist, made sure I had tons of press coverage. "The Bitch Is Back: Eileen Fulton Returns to the Stage!" the headlines read. In the show, Kay has been away from the nightclub scene for a long time. She makes her first appearance draped in a yellow feather boa, holding a long cigarette holder. She gazes at the audience, twirls the boa, and begins singing "Hello New York City! I'm back!" The audience went wild that first night because it had a special meaning for me: I was back in New York and on *World* and in a play.

The only way I managed to get through that first performance was on sheer adrenalin. I had the script backstage the whole time, trying to remember where to run, which scene was next, was I supposed to change my costume or wig—or both? The singers and dancers, who had been performing *Nightclub* for almost two years, were very supportive. They helped get me through that first nerve-racking week, which was an actor's nightmare, but, in time, it became one of my most enjoyable experiences in the theater.

I expanded upon my talents as an actress and began writing a column called "No Soap" for Rhona Barrett's *Daytime*. It was a parody at first: I would take an outrageous or obscene fan letter I had received and then answer it by writing a nasty, scathing response. What follows is a collection of some of my favorite letters from the column:

Dear Eileen:

I have always loved and respected you until I saw a picture of you revealing a lot of cleavage. Who do you think you are? You are on a respectable show, but I no longer respect you!

Disgusted

The letter was accompanied by a picture. The sender had drawn a circle around my neckline so I would be sure to know what he or she meant.

Dear Disgusted:

How I wish you had chosen a better name for yourself! I love low-necked dresses, turtleneck dresses, backless dresses, and strapless dresses. The picture certainly did not reveal me topless! The dress I wore was a bit revealing and, hopefully, a bit sexy.

What you *really* saw, and what you *thought* you saw, are two (please pardon the pun) different things. I congratulate you on possessing a fantastic imagination.

Dear Eileen:

I read where people don't like you because you are a pig on TV. You are so nosy you mind everybody else's business but your own. The writer should kick you off the show. I hope Natalie Chapman and Jay Cooney hate you in real life. If you are really like that, you will never have a friend.

Concerned

Dear Concerned:

I belong to the "Homo sapiens" species. I am not a pig. I'm thankful for the lovely friends I have and I'm delighted I have been so convincing on the show!

Dear Mrs. Fulton:

I think that Joyce Coleman is far more beautiful than you. Why don't you give up and scrape off your makeup so your jowls can fall, and the wrinkles can sag! After all, you are a mother of a 40-year-old son!

A Male Viewer

Dear MV:

If there were such a cream or makeup that would keep the jowls from sagging—the wrinkles from view—please tell us gals! I'm obviously in the wrong business, and NO WAY could I, Eileen Fulton, have a 40-year-old son.

P.S. You are right, however. Joyce Coleman, played by Barbara Rodell, is beautiful.

Dear Eileen Fulton:

What is the first thing you notice about a man?

Inquisitive

Dear Inquisitive:

*One* of the first things I notice is his hands. Are they clean? Are his nails dirty or bitten away? Hands tell a lot about a person.

Dear Eileen:

I am 20 years old. I want to have my face lifted. I've heard pros and cons about this. What would you suggest?

Unsure

Dear Unsure:

First of all—what's wrong with your face? Look in the mirror, because you may have a very special, unique face. Here are some BAD reasons for a face lift:

1. To keep my husband.
2. To change my life.
3. To look a lot younger.

You must realize whatever changes you do to your face won't change the inner you. Be sure you love who you are first. Consult with a reputable doctor, then see another doctor (always get two opinions!). Personally, I think you're much too young.

Dear Ms. Fulton:

I hate soap operas! I hate all they stand for, and I hate the idea that my mother is so stuck on your show. And, to my horror, so are my kids. I have therefore been forced to see a little of it—and, yes, you are good—but you are wasting your time and talent. I have seen you on stage. Why don't you liberate yourself from the drudgery of soaps? Do some worthwhile things with your talent!

Nell

Dear Nell:

Thank you for the compliments on my being an entertainer. I love nothing more than a live audience, but please have some respect for daytime drama. Obviously, you haven't really had time to watch enough or fully understand our show. There are quite a few good actors on it, and some truly wonderful scenes. We are a dedicated bunch. We work very hard, and it does pay off.

Dear Eileen:

Why don't they ever let soap opera characters be happy? Does it hurt?

Unhappy

Dear Unhappy:

You bet! They used to say, "Laugh, and the ratings go down." However, a lot more humor is creeping (thank heavens!) into the shows. That's important, since it's certainly human to laugh as well as to cry. But it's true, we can't have an interesting show if everyone is happy and carefree.

Dear Eileen:

Enough about babies! It seems everyone wants a baby and can't have one, or doesn't want a baby and then gets "knocked-up." Don't your writers know that women want more than babies? And why must they always show a career woman who is a pure witch? Career women can be good people! They, too, can get together over cocktails or a cup of tea and discuss love, sex, the current story line. Get with the times!

Fed Up

Dear Fed Up:

In so many ways I agree with you. I also am concerned that on some shows (not all) a woman wanting a career is portrayed as a scheming, hard-driving, unloving human being. As far as more babies or fewer babies, if you have read the papers or followed the news, you will realize that there are women who do want children.

Dear Eileen:

You went to the White House! How exciting! Did you take pictures? Please tell me all about it. Oh, how I wish I could go there, too. What an honor!

A Patriot

This particular reader was referring to an article about several soap opera actors who had been invited to the White House when Jimmy Carter was president. In the fall of 1978, Joyce Becker and Allan Sugarman had organized a Soap Opera Festival in Washington, D.C. They had arranged for a group of daytime's favorite performers to be honored guests at the White House.

It was a hot, muggy afternoon. Our group consisted of about fourteen people—actors (Susan Lucci, Jim Pritchett, and Dorothy Malone), writers, members of the USO, and a retired colonel and his wife. It took three limousines to get us there. Once we pulled up in front of the White House, enormous iron gates remained closed until our identification had been carefully scrutinized. We were then issued an orange and white card to pin on and escorted inside. We were taken on a special tour by President Carter's sons, Chip and Jeff, and shown rooms not generally seen by the public.

The Oval Office was overwhelming. It was smaller, brighter, and more cheerful than I had imagined. All of the windows had about four inches of bulletproof glass for protection.

As we toured the house, my imagination went into overdrive, picturing all of the famous events that had taken place through the years. To smell the embers from the fireplace (of the "fireside chats" fame) and to feel the soft cushion of grass under my feet in the exquisite rose garden, where so many wonderful men and women had stood, was magical, indeed. The most impressive part of the house was the Eleanor Roosevelt Room. A large portrait of her hung opposite the door as you walked in. The room was painted in a soft green-gray, with an impressive oriental rug in the middle of the floor. The walls were lined with gold and silver objects and tokens given her from all over the world for her great work and compassion. I loved it. Anyone who visits our nation's capital should take the time for a tour of this great house.

After a few months of writing my column, I decided not only would I answer some of the letters but I would write useful information about health and hygiene as well. I would pick a particular part of the body and then offer my tips—in an amusing fashion, of course. One column was about feet: "Now, men," it began, "don't stop reading. This may be a beauty hint but you've got feet, too." Or, "This month's column is all about legs: you must moisturize your legs every day or your skin will shrivel up and drop off by the end of the day! And men, you've got to do it, too. It's so embarrassing when you take off your socks or trousers and that dry white skin just flakes to the floor. You don't want dandruff on your knees. So don't be bashful, boys: Lubricate those legs and soften that skin!"

The next month, I decided to really be bold. I wrote a column about genital hygiene. The editorial staff loved it but refused to publish the piece as written. They did, however, post it on the bulletin board for everyone to read. I didn't think it was so outrageous. I wrote, "You've got to be very careful with deodorant soaps when you're washing your private parts. Men and women, take heed: Some of those soaps are very harsh on tender skin which (hopefully) doesn't get exposed to the sun very often. You can develop painful and unsightly rashes and your sweetheart is not going to believe you when you blame it on the wash. Why, you could bust up a good relationship over a cake of soap!" I tried to convince the editors that the readers would just laugh at the whole thing, but I went unpublished that month! I continued to write the column for a couple of years.

Although my career as a writer didn't exactly skyrocket, a few years later I was asked to write a brief article for the *National Lampoon*'s "Mad as Hell" issue. The assignment was to write in five hundred words or less about a topic that made me "mad as hell." I had been complaining for years about the fact that the studio is so overly air-conditioned I feel like a popsicle, so I wrote an article entitled "Nipples," which read as follows:

It's so cold in the CBS studios that your nipples stand up like a Christmas tree. It's terribly embarrassing. If anyone wants to make a porno movie they should rent the CBS studio for a day—it will save the actors from having to use ethyl chloride or pinching their little titties to make their nipples stand out. You don't even have to take your clothes off: it's so cold in the CBS studios you could wear a three-piece wool suit and you'd still look like you were over excited. This is very inconvenient when you're working for a wholesome P&G [Proctor & Gamble] show because they don't even want anyone to know you have nipples. If it happens, they summon the wardrobe mistress and make her put band aids across your private parts and then you have little squares sticking out on your chest which looks even worse.

And what if you're doing a breakfast scene with your mother-in-law and your little nipples start rising up from beneath that flower-patterned housecoat. Of course, *you* know it's because your freezing to death but the audience might think you've got the hots for your mama which will just detract from the scene. So what are you supposed to do? To avoid the band aids you can hide behind one of the sets, pull your top off and blow warm wonderful air down your front; then rub those cold mounds of flesh real hard with your palms to take the chill off. But you have to be careful when you do it because if the crew catches you they're just going to think you're doing something nasty and then there goes your reputation. So really, what's a respectable but freezing actress supposed to do?

I got paid $250 for that piece. When I first submitted it one of the editors came to the studio to see if I was a lunatic—or maybe they thought they'd see some nipples. I don't know what they decided once they met me, but the article was published as written. They used a picture of me dressed in a fur coat and big mittens. I got a lot of press—and mail—from that article.

A few years later, I was in an elevator at CBS and a gentleman turned around and stared at me.

"You're Eileen Fulton, aren't you?"

"Yes."

"You wrote that article about the air-conditioning for the *Lampoon,* didn't you?"

I nodded.

"You still freezing on the set?"

I felt like saying why don't you stop by and see for yourself, but I was in a "good-girl" mood, so I just smiled and said, "Yes."

"Well, I'm in charge of all the air-conditioning at CBS. I've got that article still hanging on my wall downstairs. Just about everyone in this building has teased me about that piece. I was going to write an article for the *Lampoon* saying I was "mad as hell" about what you wrote for the "mad as hell" issue but I'm over it. You're a very funny writer."

I became involved with NOW (the National Organization for Women) during the mid-eighties. I was always very supportive of the women's movement and the Equal Rights Amendment. Ever since I was a little girl, I believed in equal pay for equal ability. I remember overhearing a conversation between two neighbors when I was in the third grade. They were upset because one of the mothers was stirring up trouble: She found out a male schoolteacher was making more than Mrs. Wilson—an instructor who was considered one of the best in the school system. I was curious and interrupted the conversation.

"Why does Mr. Jenkins make more?" I asked.

"Well, he's a man, dear."

"Isn't Mrs. Wilson a good teacher?"

"She's the best we have, but that's not the point."

"Is Mr. Jenkins a good schoolteacher?"

"He's just fine—not great but fine."

"So why should he get more?"

"He's the head of a household."

I was an inquisitive child with a logical mind. I just kept firing questions until something made sense.

"But Mrs. Wilson's husband died and she's got a little boy so isn't *she* the head of *her* household? Shouldn't she get the same money?"

My neighbors were tired of playing "Humor the Kid." "Margaret go on home and stop asking so many silly questions. You're just too young to understand!"

I felt adamant about it then and my convictions only strengthened in time. When the national campaign began for the ratification of the ERA, I felt compelled to get involved in some capacity. I telephoned the president of NOW at the time, Ellie Smeal, and volunteered my services.

"I have a large audience of people who listen to what I say. I think I could be a positive influence and teach people what NOW is all about."

"Eileen, we'd love to have you on board."

"I need to find out more about the organization so I'll know what I'm talking about. Could we arrange a time for me to come to Washington and meet with you?"

Ellie telephone a few days later. She had organized a one-day conference in Washington and had invited a variety of high-profile women to discuss the objectives of the organization and how to communicate that message to a wider audience. Some of the women in attendance were concerned because I was involved with the March of Dimes: They felt that MOD's position on abortion was inconsistent with NOW's and utilizing me as a spokesperson for the two groups might pose a problem. I told them they were misinformed. Having traveled all over the country for the organization, meeting patients, doctors, and pregnant women, I had learned that one of MOD's concerns was helping women have healthy babies, but they certainly weren't against birth control.

I originally began working with charity organizations by hosting or performing on telethons. Dori's brother had cerebral palsy and she hooked me up with local chapters to assist with the never-ending but nevertheless crucial task of fund-raising. I traveled to various locations around the country and hosted and sang at telethons. A few years later I hooked up with MOD. In 1985, I had the privilege of hosting the first international MOD telethon, which was broadcast from Atlantic City. I kept changing my hair and my clothes, singing songs and interviewing guests. The audience was wonderful and I really enjoyed myself.

I interviewed a darling and precious "dirt shy" young boy named Matt Dillon (I didn't know who he was at the time—I just thought he was cute and very polite). I found out it was Matt's birthday, so I told the viewers that they should get on the phone, make a pledge, and wish this cute young boy a "Happy Birthday."

Later that year, I was honored to receive the Caring American Award from The Ladies Auxiliary of The Veteran's of Foreign War. I flew to Dallas to attend the convention and was quite honored by the occasion and the award. One of the most satisfying things a recognizable personality can do is use his or her celebrity status to assist charitable organizations or spread a little hope and cheer to those in need. Fame is really a gift: We can work very hard to be the best, but we really have little control over whether or not that work is acknowledged on a national or international level. And like any gift, whether it's a glorious voice, the rock-steady hands of a surgeon, or a teacher's innate ability to inspire, it is up to each of us to decide how to use our gifts.

I think most celebrities would agree that after a while it's not satisfying enough to use fame just to serve yourself. At some point, there is a need to give something back—to make a contribution whether it's financial, emotional, or spiritual.

I heard about the nonprofit organization "Hearts & Voices" and met its founder, Nancy Sondag. The group organizes live performances aimed at easing the loneliness and suffering of hospitalized individuals suffering from AIDS. I wanted to do something to cheer up the patients, so Nancy arranged for me to sing a few songs in one of the hospitals. They were so sweet. Some of them apologized for not feeling up to attending the performance, but they told me they would keep their doors open to listen.

There was one patient in particular who was so positive—so affirming—he hadn't given up on himself. He told me he looked forward to the day when he would get out of the hospital, sit in the park, and just look at the sky. This man tried to inspire the other patients with his optimistic attitude and outlook—to live life to the fullest, one day at a time. It's the strongest memory I took away from that experience, and it is one I try to remember, even today. "One day at a time"—it almost sounds like the title of a new daytime soap, but it's just so true.

I loved having a house in Connecticut where I could escape Manhattan's never-ending motion and madness. It's one of the most exciting cities in the world, but you have to find a place where you can catch your breath. Connecticut proved to be the perfect resting place for me. Rather than drive myself into the city each day, I decided to use a limousine service, and it came equipped with a cute, muscular driver named Chad. He was a six-foot, blond-haired, blue-eyed boy from the South, and I thought he was just adorable. Everyone has a weakness: Some people like sweets—I like "sweet men with dimples."

After about a month of driving me between New York and Connecticut, Chad tried to convince me that it would be more economical if I hired him full-time and purchased my own car. I ran the idea past my accountant, and he thought it was a financially sound one. Before I had made my final decision, however, something happened that convinced me to hire Chad: I started receiving death threats again. Chad could not only be my chauffeur, he would also make the perfect bodyguard. I had a basement apartment in my house and, living alone in Connecticut, I knew I would feel safer if there was someone else in the house. When I presented the idea to Chad, he jumped at the opportunity.

My life was once again in jeopardy because of the infamous "Grandmother Clause" in my contract. Back in the seventies, when the writers decided Tom, my soap son, was going to marry Carol, I objected very vigorously.

"Look, I don't mind if you want to marry him off but he can't become a legitimate father. *I* can't become a grandmother!"

"Really, Eileen, we're not certain what's going to happen, but we don't think it's up to you to make that decision."

I was furious. Ten minutes later I had Irna on the phone. I knew she would tell me the truth.

"Irna, I trust you. Are you going to make me a grandmother?"

"Of course we are."

That's all I needed to know. I wasn't refusing to become a grandmother out of pure vanity. My story line was running hot and heavy with Michael Shea. Would the audience accept a seductive, conniving, sexy vixen who had to baby-sit for her new grandchild? More important, would the story line be dropped because of an impending grandchild? I felt at the time that the writers had a preconceived notion of how grandparents behaved. They didn't know how to create interesting story lines for them.

Based on what I had observed through the years, I believed they thought grandmothers were people who made cookies, poured milk, and sat in rocking chairs offering sage advice. I was convinced they would take away Lisa's love life—her sex life—which would alter the character completely. It was just a matter of time before they would be ordering me to store away the sequins and fetch the flannel. After all, look what happened to Claire Cassen on *World*. They aged her children and turned her grandchildren into adults overnight, making her a great-grand-mother at thirty-nine, and then hit her with a truck!

Although the situation has improved somewhat since then, writers and producers still want to take the sex out of *sex*-agenarian. If you look at most of the grandparents depicted in films or on television today, you'll find a collection of nice, safe, sexless senior citizens. If there are scenes with citizens over sixty in bed together, it's usually treated in a comedic—not a natu-ral—manner, as if the situation is so outrageous it has to be funny. Perhaps the creative industry is just reflecting what they believe to be the attitudes of the society. I just wish someone had the nerve to create a sexy, glamorous, seductive, *hot* grand-mother who didn't have to apologize or feel embarrassed about the fact that she was still celebrating life in every possible way. Instead of "Auntie Mame" I could be "Granny Mame"!

When they originally tried to make Lisa a grandmother, however, I was forced to put my foot down. My contract was up for renewal, and my popularity was running high. I used these two factors to my advantage.

It's childish to give producers an ultimatum unless you be-lieve so strongly in your demands that you're prepared to walk away. In this particular case, I had no doubts. I called a meeting with the producers and writers and told them straight out, "If you make me a grandmother I won't renew. There will be no point because you will have destroyed the character. I'm sorry, but that's the way I feel." In a matter of days, Tom's new wife, Carol, became "Sterile-Carol." The problem was resolved—at least for a while. From that point on, every time Tom got married, something would happen to his wife. It was always the poor wife.

In the eighties, when Tom and Margo got married and Margo was pregnant, the actor who played Tom at the time decided to leave the show. The only way the producers could dissolve the relationship was to have Margo lose the baby. Many of the viewers, who were aware of my "Granny Clause," blamed *me* for Margo's miscarriage! I began receiving the most terrifying mail of my career. "You horrible bitch!" one letter began. "You baby-killer! I don't know how you can live with yourself!" Letters poured into the network and the studio. A few of the writers stated that they were going to "kill the baby-killer!"

Death threats should always be taken seriously. Sadly, the atmosphere of terror has only increased after the tragic deaths of such celebrities as Rebecca Schaeffer and John Lennon. For the first time in my life, I was frightened some crazed viewer might actually kill me because of a change in the story line. I felt I really needed protection and welcomed having a handsome driver who could also double as my bodyguard.

Chad, like many of the men in my life, became overly possessive and protective. I don't know if it was out of a sincere affection for me or if he just didn't want anyone else influencing my decisions, but Chad became visibly irritated when I was in the company of other men. It wasn't as if he had become my sole advisor, but when you spend several hours a day with some-

one in a confined space like a car, you start talking. Especially if
that driver is a good listener. I began confiding in Chad, narrat-
ing my problems out loud, as if I were in a therapy session.

While I appreciated his "ear," I didn't welcome his interfer-
ence. On several occasions when I was entertaining potential
"boyfriends," Chad would charge into the living room eyes
blazing and muscles bulging at the most inopportune moments
and act as if I were being attacked by a mad rapist. It was very
embarrassing to say the least.

I had given up my New York apartment when I was living
in Los Angeles, so whenever I had to stay overnight in Manhattan, I booked a room at The Regency. They were always so
kind and sweet and I always felt protected, which was very important to me at the time. And they had wonderful little ameni-
ties like orchids in the bathrooms. Because I was spending a
small fortune on hotel bills, my business manager suggested it
might be wise to purchase an apartment in the city. One day, I
was in the car with my press agent, David, discussing my hous-
ing dilemma. He suggested we visit the site of a marvelous new
high-rise that was being constructed across the street from
where he lived.

I thought it sounded like fun and asked Chad to drive us to
the designated address. He got just furious about the whole
thing. I think Chad was secure living in the house and felt
threatened that I wouldn't need him if I spent more time in the
city. He certainly wouldn't have the opportunity to listen to me
talking about my life and troubles. In retrospect, I think Chad
believed that David was trying to get me away from him. The
moment I asked him to take us to the site, he flew into a rage.
He made a wild turn and we almost got clobbered by another
vehicle. Of course he apologized profusely, but it was evident
that he didn't want to drive me to see the apartment building.

We went anyway, and it was breathtaking. I put on a hard

hat and rode the construction elevator up to the thirty-sixth floor. The wind was blowing, the sky was vibrant, and the views were unparalleled. I hung on to a steel girder, my knees shaking, and yelled to all the world to hear, "I'll take it!"

Like a bizarre plot line out of *World,* my life veered off in a direction I never would have anticipated: I fell in love and began to have an affair with a married man. Being a high-profile individual who attracted the attention of the public and the press, I had to be very careful and *very* discreet about my dangerous liaison. I had doubts about what I was doing the entire time, but my sense of loneliness and passionate feelings for the gentleman overrode any sense of logic or reason. He was Catholic and unable to get a divorce from his unhappy situation. Approximately two years into my affair, I began to experience terrible abdominal pains, so I went to the doctor and was devastated when he told me what was wrong.

"Eileen, we won't know for sure until the tests come back, but I think you're pregnant."

I was fifty-four years old! How could I possibly be pregnant? If it was a scene on a soap, it certainly would have been the Friday cliff-hanger.

# ELEVEN

# "Let's Get Married," I Said

$\mathcal{B}$efore I had a chance to even catch my breath, the doctor snatched the possibility of motherhood away from me as quickly as he had tossed it in the air.

"If you are pregnant," he said as he handed me a glass of water, "it's in the tubes and we'll have to terminate the pregnancy and perform a hysterectomy. But let's find out if you're pregnant first."

I couldn't begin to absorb all of the information. First I might be having a baby, then I was going to have to give up the baby, and then I could never have a child again! I remember thinking how awful it was to have come so close to becoming a mother and to have to then give up the child. I was very much in love and I knew this was the only child I would ever carry. Because of my nonstop career demands and my unsuccessful marriages, I had never really focused on starting a family. Being so close to it, so late in life, just overwhelmed me. I immediately telephoned my best friend and confidante—my mother—and, as always, she was very understanding and supportive.

"Sweetie, just remember, whatever happens I love you and I'm here for you."

The next day I was at Dr. Marbach's office for regular treatment when I telephoned my gynecologist for the test results.

"Hello," I said as my entire body trembled violently. I was ready to slam down the receiver and wait until I was in the privacy of my own home, but was too anxious. I had to know. Now. I decided to sit down.

"Hello?"

"Yes. This is Eileen Fulton."

"Oh, you're the one who's having twins, aren't you?" the nurse replied.

"Twins! Oh, no! At least I don't think so. I'm calling to find out if I'm pregnant or not," I said hesitantly. There was a pause for a few seconds while she retrieved the correct file. I remember hearing someone in the background ordering lunch and thought how strange it all was—life-altering events mixed up with everyday occurrences.

"Hello? Hello? Are you still there?" the woman asked.

I had drifted off again into the moving pictures of my imagination, painting images of myself pushing a stroller or cradling a child. "Yes. I'm here. I'm listening."

"Don't worry, Mrs. Fulton. You're fine," she said matter-of-factly. "Not pregnant but just fine."

The voice tore right through me as if my almost child had suddenly been ripped from my body. I dropped the telephone receiver and began sobbing uncontrollably. The receptionist asked if I needed help.

"No, thanks, I'm fine," I whispered, thinking *I'm not fine at all*. "I just got some bad news, that's all."

"Can I get you anything, Miss Fulton?"

"No, really. I just need to catch my breath."

When Chad picked me up I broke down all over again in the car. After I calmed myself, I began telling him exactly what had happened: my affair with the married man, the false pregnancy, everything. I really needed to talk to someone and Chad was there. Unfortunately, he was disgusted and appalled by my story. Instead of sympathy, he offered silence. He disapproved of my indiscretions and obviously felt I got what I deserved.

For days I thought about whether I had missed out in life by not having children. I remembered how I helped my mother raise Jimmy and Charles. I certainly felt like I was both sister and "little mom" to them when we were growing up. And I've had such wonderful experiences being a television mother to all the Toms and Chuckys and Scotts who have appeared on *World*. Some actors are thrown by working with kids because they're so unpredictable, but I've always loved it.

Gary Schaeffer was the first of my Toms, but when the producers decided to have my son start school, they had to hire an older actor. Frankie Michaels replaced Gary. Frankie used to get nervous about forgetting a line, so I'd take him aside and say, "Now, Frankie, don't you worry. It doesn't matter if you don't say it exactly the way it's written. You just talk to me and we'll have such fun. Now let's go play!" Frankie was a remarkably talented young actor who loved the world of make-believe. He worked on our show for several years, and I felt privileged being able to watch him grow up while playing his television mom.

After days of mind-wrestling, I finally decided that even though I had never had a child of my own, I was not totally deprived of a mother's experiences. Whether it was through the nurturing of my brothers or the interaction with all of my soap sons, or even the love and affection I've shared with my dogs, I have had moments where I definitely felt like a mother. I decided to stop feeling sorry for myself and get on with my life.

When I told my secret love about the false pregnancy, he was gentle and tender. He held me and we cried together for our child that might have been. It was becoming increasingly difficult to see each other: He did love his children and wanted to spend time with them. I lived in the public eye surrounded by reporters or photographers who always wanted to know what I was up to. After a very long and heart-felt discussion, we both decided it was time to end our affair. In less than a week, I had lost a child and a lover.

My relationship with Chad continued to deteriorate. After he was so judgmental about my false pregnancy, I didn't feel the same about him. He interfered more and more in my personal life and began abusing his house and car privileges. I think the conclusive factor that finally influenced my decision to fire him was the fact that I no longer felt like my life was in danger. The death threats and hate mail had long since stopped. Those crazed fans had probably moved on to terrorize some other poor actor with some other new plot line.

Having endured such a painful experience I felt stronger—less vulnerable. It had taken me years to figure out, but I finally learned I had to get rid of the men who detracted from my life and used me. I seem to give them too much rope and then find out I'm on the short end.

One morning in Connecticut, I finally confronted Chad and told him that it was time for us to part company. He was shocked. Tears and anger flooded his face, but he left that very day. I telephoned the security company and had them change the locks and codes on all of the doors and windows. A few days later the alarms started going off in the middle of the night. Chad had arrived and decided to let himself in by jimmying one of the sliding doors. His belongings were still in the basement and I had wondered when he would be arriving to get them back, but I hardly expected a house call at 3 A.M.

When I confronted him, he told me that he had spoken to a lawyer, and, based on some bizarre Connecticut law regarding squatters' rights, he was legally entitled to live in the house for as long as he wanted to. It was the most ridiculous thing I had heard in a long time. My lawyers checked it out and told me it was true: squatters' rights, which Chad's lawyer wanted a large sum of money in exchange for his relinquishing. I had already given him two weeks severance, which I felt was fair enough considering the circumstances. Every night at exactly 3 A.M., Chad and his lawyer would arrive, let themselves in, drink beer, make a lot of noise, and then leave. They were obviously harassing me so that I'd pay Chad whatever he wanted. Eventually we settled out of court for a small sum.

I'm always grateful for the fact that whenever my personal life is in turmoil, I can at least go to work, "be" someone else, and forget my troubles for a few hours a day. One of the more interesting on-screen intrigues I became involved with during this period centered around an interracial romance and the prejudice it aroused. Ironically, Lisa—one of the most outgoing, liberal-minded characters on the show—was forced to confront her own prejudices.

Our executive producer, Laurence Caso, came up with the idea. He said he wanted to do a story line about racial prejudice and thought it would be fascinating to have Lisa be opposed to an interracial marriage as a way of demonstrating that people who say "I'm not prejudiced" often are when confronted with a particular situation. Doug Marland wrote wonderful scenes that depicted all the different points of view. I hated playing it on a personal level, because it was articulating something I felt strongly about, but as an actress it was a great opportunity.

Some people really *are* blind to their own prejudice, and, in this instance, Lisa was definitely guilty—she could understand the love interest between Duncan, who was Caucasian, and Jessica, who was African-American, but she opposed the marriage. Of course, Lisa eventually learned to overcome her old way of thinking. She eventually became the godmother of Duncan and Jessica's child.

In 1988, I was absolutely thrilled to learn that Farley Granger had been hired to play Earl Mitchell, the latest in a long line of Lisa's husbands. Ever since I was a young girl I had had a crush on him. Years ago, when I lived in Marion, North Carolina, my friends and I went to see *The Hatfields and McCoys* starring Farley. He played the young Hatfield boy who fell in love with Roseanna McCoy.

In the film, there was a scene in which he whistles like a whippoorwill for his love. She runs into the woods and he suddenly appears from behind a bush and grabs her. She initially resists him but then succumbs to his passionate kisses. He eventually carries her behind a bush while the whippoorwills cry, and the whole scene fades to black.

When the sun rises in the next scene, the young couple emerge from behind the bush, fastening buttons, adjusting clothing. It was hot! We were little girls, but we thought we knew what was going on and it was enough to get us excited. Every afternoon after school, we went to see the movie while it was playing in town just to live through that scene again and again.

I dressed especially with Farley in mind for his first day on the set, wearing a lovely black dress accessorized by two strings of long pearls. The moment I laid eyes on my matinee idol, I ran to the chair where he was seated, threw myself into his lap, and began singing the title song, "Roseanna, Roseanna, Roseanna McCoy . . ."

"Eileen, I can't believe anyone could remember that horrible, horrible movie," he laughed.

It may have been horrible to him, but for a group of adolescent girls in Marion, it was absolutely scintillating. Whenever anyone asks me for my idea of a love or sex scene, I tell them about Farley Granger in *The Hatfields and McCoys*.

We worked together for about a year and a half until they killed poor Earl Mitchell by smothering him with a pillow.

When I first laid eyes on Rick—the gentleman who was to become Husband No. 3—I thought he had a wife. After my last experience dating a married man, I decided to avoid anyone with a wedding band. I was the honorary chairman at one of those political benefits where all you do is smile and greet people, hoping they'll all write a big check by the end of the evening. There was a very attractive man seated next to a beautiful woman, and I just assumed they were husband and wife. They were just the cutest couple. It wasn't until a year later, at the same annual fundraiser, that I found out the lovely woman was Rick's sister. He was free and clear. I could feel my hormones kick in as I began actively flirting with him.

A few weeks later a friend, Dee, arranged for mutual friends of ours, Denise and Ted Lovegrove, to invite Rick, his sister, and me to a Valentine's Day dinner. They felt Rick and I were a match made in heaven and were all dying to play Cupid. Rick and I hit it off from the start. I thought, *This man's for me.* He was available, had a sense of humor, and we could be seen in public (unlike my previous beau). He had a great job as a landscape architect and, to my surprise and delight, played the drums. How could it possibly go wrong?

How indeed! It was a whirlwind courtship and marriage. My affair with Rick was impulsive, I admit. I frequently refer to my third marriage as the "minute wedding." When I told everyone on *World* I was getting married again, Don Hastings laughed and said, "Eileen, you are the only woman I know with a wash-and-wear wedding dress!"

I wasn't really looking for a husband, but I'm very romantic and I certainly got caught up in the spirit of Valentine's Day. And with so many of my friends playing Cupid and shooting arrows at me, it was either fall in love and get married or drop dead. Rick was very old-fashioned. Yes, I still had a soft spot for men with manners. He took me to beautiful restaurants and fancy parties and always arrived with a bouquet of flowers.

It wasn't long before we both decided we were madly in love with each other. One particular evening, we were invited to join two of our biggest matchmakers, Bill and Dee Cox, for a romantic dinner at The Silvermine Tavern in Connecticut. It was a warm spring evening, and I wore a form-fitting black silk dress that showed off my hourglass figure. Rick gave me an old-fashioned movie star corsage made up of gardenias. It was supposed to be worn draped over and across the shoulder. (I always called those types of corsages "movie star" because when I was a little girl, I had a Shirley Temple book and one of the actresses pictured wore an arrangement of flowers over her shoulder.)

I decided that night—with a little prompting from Dee— that I would marry Rick. Three weeks later, I popped the question myself. Denise had organized a larger-than-life surprise birthday party for her husband. Three enormous tents had been erected on the back lawn. Pretty little pink-and-white lights twinkled over our heads. It was like living in a fairy tale. Once again, I got so caught up with the magic of the evening, I couldn't contain myself. While we were dancing, I leaned into Rick and whispered in his ear.

"Let's get married."

He just smiled and said "Okay."

It was that simple. We made the announcement that night and began planning a wedding the next day.

As was the case with my first husband, Bill, it wasn't long before I began to have serious doubts about going through with the ceremony. It seemed less and less like the right thing to do. I'm a spontaneous, romantic individual. When I love someone, I commit everything I am and everything I have to that relationship. It's taken me a lifetime to learn that you don't necessarily have to marry all the men you love. The more I thought about it, the less certain I became that Rick and I could merge lives.

I'm the first one to admit that living with an actress is not for everyone. It's a crazy, chaotic life where people are constantly in your face demanding something. There were more important concerns, however. One worry was about the amount of alcohol Rick and I consumed when we were together—was it as innocent as it seemed at the time? I realized that Rick never accompanied me to New York—had never intersected my life in the city or at the studio—and when I was in Manhattan I didn't drink. But the moment I walked through the front door of my house, Rick would be waiting with a pitcher of martinis. We would share a bottle of wine with dinner. The eighties perception of alcohol consumption was very different than it is today. At the time, our behavior appeared normal, but I grew increasingly uncomfortable with the situation.

Although my friends in Connecticut had earned their Cupid's wings bringing Rick and me together, my social circle in Manhattan felt I was rushing into another potentially disastrous marriage. My lawyer's professional opinion was "Eileen, you must be out of your mind!" I was so impetuous, I never even bothered to finalize the prenuptial agreement. I really didn't give anyone a chance to try to talk me out of it, because I knew they *could*. In retrospect, I think that it was more infatuation than love, although I believe that Rick truly loved me.

The night before the wedding, I had my entire family over for dinner. I could tell right away my brother Jimmy did not like what was going on. He has a clear-cut, practical way of looking at things and saw right off the bat that Rick and I were not a healthy combination. I decided to "loosen up the gang" with several rounds of martinis, but, of course, that only aggravated an already tense situation. During dinner I told a risqué joke and Jimmy thought it was rude because my mother was present.

"I don't have to listen to this," he snapped as he pushed

himself away from the table. Jimmy was so aggravated he accidentally knocked his chair over and stepped on my dog Sarah. Lala, my male Shitzu, was so upset he bit Sisi, my baby Shitzu. It was chaos. I was slightly drunk, overtired, and out of control. I raced after my brother, screaming and crying: "How can you act like this in my house! You come back here and apologize! Come back!"

It didn't take me long to realize that I was frustrated and fearful of the wedding. I was unfairly venting on Jimmy, but I couldn't stop myself. I thought we should just have a big cook out instead of a wedding. A simple celebration of two people being in love. Dear God, how I wish I had had the nerve to say that then. I was so close to doing it.

My mother calmed me down and put a cool cloth on my head and my brother Charles rubbed my back. "I've seen this before, Sweetie," she said. "Alcoholism runs in our family."

I felt like someone had switched the channel and suddenly I was thrust into the middle of someone else's plot line. "What! Mama, you can't be serious," I sobbed. "You're just upset."

"Darling, if you're not already, you're close to becoming one. Do you know your Uncle Tokie and my father and your daddy's grandfather were alcoholics? You have it coming at you from both sides of the family. You've got to watch yourself. I don't want you to ever drink again. Please, Sweetie, you've got too much to lose and I love you too much."

I was floored. I thought about that conversation all night and apologized to everyone the next day. I made a vow to clean up my act right then and there.

Rick and I invited approximately twenty-five relatives and close friends to share in our wedding celebration. I was still trying to buck tradition. Instead of a wedding cake we had a birthday cake for my cook, Annette. She was a dear, sweet lady who moved in after Chad moved out. Her birthday happened to be the exact date of the wedding, so instead of the usual "Congratulations Rick and Eileen," the cake said "Happy Birthday Annette."

I wore a very sexy dress I had purchased before I even met Rick—a delicate white crocheted creation you could see through. It featured little pearls and tiny iridescent sequins. When I tried it on for Dee Dee she raved.

"Eileen, it's gorgeous. It looks just like a wedding dress."

"You're right, but where's the groom? I'm going to have to find a husband just to wear the dress."

I met Rick a few weeks later.

My crocheted wedding dress obviously needed a slip—I wasn't *that* daring, so I bought a very expensive Christian Dior pale lavender one with lots of lace and flowers. I wore a white satin Chanel bow in my hair, which, at that point, was Afro styled and not my favorite color. I had purchased the wrong bottle of hair color the week before and had dyed my hair burgundy instead of brown.

All of the guests gathered on the outdoor deck of my house. Dee Dee and Rick's sister, Cathy, were my co-matrons of honor. Dee Dee's husband, Bill, was a justice of the peace and he performed the ceremony with the assistance of our minister, Walt Everett. Miss Frankie, my publicist David Granoff, and my handsome driver George all came.

In the midst of our celebration, we noticed that we were all getting peppered by little black specks falling from the sky. I looked up into the trees and realized they were in the middle of a gypsy moth infestation—we were all being sprinkled by worm poop! I quickly herded my guests indoors, smiling and making light of the entire event. But somehow I couldn't stop wondering if it just wasn't another awful omen.

In a matter of days, my relationship with Rick became strained because of my "No-Drinking" policy. I wasn't telling him what to do, of course. I'm not the type to leap into the preacher's pulpit and start sermonizing about the road to hell being paved with empty martini glasses. I just knew *I* had to stop. Although it hadn't reached the point where it affected my work—I never drank when I was at the studio or performing anywhere—I didn't want the problem to escalate any further. My new husband was not pleased with my decision. Like many individuals who develop addictions, Rick was not interested in "cocktails for one."

A few weeks after our wedding, I invited everyone from the show to attend a party at Scaletta in Manhattan. We had a fabulous buffet dinner with an open bar all night. I was so busy greeting guests and having my picture taken, I didn't eat a thing. Halfway through the party, I began to notice how uncomfortable Rick was around the press and the photographers. He also seemed slightly intimidated by all of my friends from *World*.

I became worried, thinking, *This is my world—my life. What if you can't intersect it and enjoy it?* After the dinner party, I invited a few close friends to my apartment. As soon as we returned home, I asked Rick for a cola, but he insisted on serving me a martini.

"Go on, Eileen," he urged. "It's a celebration. Just have one."

"No, thanks. I haven't eaten a thing and it would go straight to my head."

He placed a martini in my hand anyway while I was talking to his sister. I remember looking down into the glass and seeing the olives. I was starved at that point, so I whisked down the martini and popped the olives in my mouth. Rick quickly replaced my drink, I downed that one too, and when I set the beautiful crystal glass on the table, I misjudged the space. The martini glass shattered. I burst into tears, realizing that I was drunk and certainly didn't want to be. I had obviously lost control of the situation. The big question was: Had I lost control of my life? I couldn't stop crying. The guests quickly left.

Rick lost his job, which only aggravated our problems. I told him not to worry, I would take care of him. Repeating patterns of the past, I thought I would put him on my payroll as the drummer in my nightclub act. I've frequently offered the men in my life jobs to give them a sense of purpose and self-worth. It rarely enhanced the relationship, and I realize now it didn't do a lot for their self-esteem. Isn't it ironic how we end up hurting the people we're trying to help?

I soon found out that Rick didn't like New York parties, the press, and other aspects of being in the public eye, all of which had become second nature to me. He hadn't been around long enough to understand what my life was about on a day-to-day basis. Reporters and journalists constantly wanted to interview and photograph Rick, but he wasn't interested. Unlike my previous husband, who loved being the center of attention, Rick was very shy. He tried to be pleasant and accomodating, but it was difficult, and he was always uncomfortable.

A few months into the marriage, Rick began to develop serious health problems—severe emphysema and then pneumonia—but he refused to stop drinking or smoking for more than a few days. It appeared to me that he was trying to destroy himself like some tragic version of *A Star Is Born*. On several occasions I tried to talk to him about what was happening, but he wouldn't listen.

"I can't believe you're afraid of having a little drink," he stated like it was a dare.

"No," I replied. "I can drink a little but I can't drink a lot. More important, I don't want to drink a lot. I know my limitations now."

Rick felt that my stance on alcohol was an act of judgment

and abandonment. I didn't want to be a part of where I thought he was going. I couldn't help him—no matter how hard I tried. In fact, I was convinced being married to me was detrimental to his health.

Based on my past relationships—both personal and professional—I had learned that it was best to terminate an unhealthy relationship as quickly as possible. Three months after I had been married, I knew it was time to pull the plug.

I was working at the studio and Rick was up at the house painting the bedroom peach—and I mean literally everything: the phone, the radio, everything he saw. He obviously was not feeling well. Rick telephoned me late in the afternoon because it was my birthday and we hadn't made plans.

"Happy birthday, darling. I'm going to have George drive me in and we'll go to a lovely restaurant," he said.

I had thought about this moment for a long time and decided I couldn't put it off any longer. "No, Rick. What I'd really like you to do for my birthday is pack your things and leave."

He was stunned and speechless.

"Rick, I'm sorry, but it's not going to work. We just can't seem to work things out. I think you know that. It really would be best for both of us in the long run if we parted company now. Please."

Rick quietly agreed to honor my request.

I really cared for Rick and didn't want to hurt him, so I made every effort to let him down gently. I explained why I felt the relationship no longer worked—why I couldn't go on living the way we were—and why I thought he would be better off *not* being married to me. He didn't fight me at all. True to form, he was a gentlemen.

My lawyer was ready to do battle at the divorce hearing because Rick had never signed a prenuptial agreement. The courtroom, with its wood paneling and benches, looked just like a television set. I wore my black "divorce suit" and a simple diamond pin. Rick represented himself. He looked quite dashing in a light blue suit that matched his eyes. The judge questioned him thoroughly to make sure he understood what his rights were.

"Do you realize that you rightfully own half of everything this woman owns?"

"Yes, sir."

"Do you realize how well off she is?"

"Yes, sir."

"And you are prepared to relinquish everything?"

There was a dramatic pause as all eyes in the court darted back and forth between Rick and me. I looked at him as he stood there all by himself. I wasn't quite certain exactly what he would say. He just winked at me and smiled.

"I don't want anything," he finally replied in a calm, gentle voice. "I love this lady and I don't want to take anything that's hers."

I thought I'd melt! It was better than anything I had ever seen or played on television. I wanted to leap into his arms, call off the whole thing, ride into the sunset, and live happily ever after. This was the kind and beautiful side of the man I had fallen in love with—the gentleman who was my hero. But then I remembered that, when he drank, a darker side emerged, and I knew I couldn't live with that. It was one of the most moving moments of my life, and it was certainly the most generous, selfless thing anyone has ever done for me.

If that's not love—what is?

The year after my divorce was a physically difficult one. I began experiencing terrible stomach pains again. One day while I was working at the studio, I couldn't even stand up. I was doubled over in my dressing room. Coleen Zank, who plays Barbara, looked in and exclaimed, "Leenie, are you okay?" Colleen is a dear friend, someone who has always been there for me. She called her doctor, and my driver, George, raced me to the hospital. The gynecologist recommended I finally have a hysterectomy. I agreed. I dreaded going back into the hospital, not so much because I was afraid of hospitals but because I always hated the loss of whatever privacy I had in my life. As I made quite clear the time I was in the emergency room and they wouldn't even let me go to the bathroom in peace, being a celebrity when you're trapped in a hospital bed is not the easiest thing in the world. You're at the mercy of whoever might pop in and ask for an autograph.

Several years ago I was in the hospital with a fever of 104 degrees. During my stay I began having what I thought were hallucinations, but my visions turned out to be quite real. At approximately 5:30 each morning, I would wake up feeling like tiny bugs were crawling all over my face. My private nurse, Maggie, thought I was hallucinating because I was running a very high fever.

"Eileen," she began while dabbing my head with a cool damp cloth, "don't worry. Nothing's crawling on your face. You're just fine."

"Tiny bugs. There must have been teensy, tiny bugs crawling on me while I was sleeping."

"Just relax," she urged in a soothing voice.

The exact same thing happened the next morning and at exactly the same time. I woke up convinced that these tiny bugs *had* been crawling around the periphery of my face. Maggie once again washed me down, assuring me that everything was all right. The third morning I felt the "bugs" again. This time, however, I woke up and saw a group of nurses huddled around my bed. They were all leaning over my body, scrutinizing my face. For a quick flash I thought they might be a coven of witches about to offer up a sacrifice. One of them carefully lifted the spit curls that framed my face and began moving her finger along the hairline.

"Look. You see," my torturer stated, "look there, and there, no scars. She hasn't had her face lifted."

I started thinking I was dead. What did she mean, "my face lifted." Was I in heaven without my head? I didn't know what was going on.

"Maybe it's not really *her!*" one of them snapped.

"Of course it's *her*," another retorted, grabbing my chart. "This is Eileen Fulton from *As the World Turns*. She's forty-one years old and she's never had a face lift. Look at that skin! She could be my daughter!"

Just then, my savior, Maggie, walked in on the "examination."

"What do you think you're doing?" she yelled. "Leave my patient alone. I can't believe you're nurses and you behave like that. Go on, get out, get out of here! Shoo!"

After the entire hospital staff heard what happened, they were all curious to see what my skin was like—everyone was dying to play the latest game, "searching for scars." Doctors, nurses, administrators all dropped in to visit me on one pretext or another, but I could always tell by the way they stared that they were probing my hairline for telltale signs of surgery.

Finally Maggie decided to put a stop to all the nonsense. She placed a large red stripe across the front of my door, which meant unauthorized personnel were not allowed to enter. On top of the ribbon she taped a sign that read: "Yes, this is Eileen Fulton. No, she has not had a facelift. Now leave her alone!"

God bless Maggie!

By the end of 1990, I decided to concentrate my professional energies on singing once again. I thought if I worked on something I loved, I would feel better—physically and mentally. I found a piano player and began putting together a new night-club act. Performing in a theater or a nightclub always revitalizes me. When it comes to those energizing "C"s of life—champagne, cocaine, and caffeine—I'll take the safest of them all: a crowd! I was thrilled to be singing in front of a live audience again.

I performed at Tatou, an elegant Manhattan club. At one point during my first set, the crowd became so noisy I couldn't even hear the band behind me. I realized I was singing one song and the boys were playing another. I thought, *Let me see if I can get this room quiet.* I walked away from the microphone and just kept talking. Everyone gradually began to grow quiet. They wondered what I was saying and what they were missing. When the room was silent, I walked back to the microphone and said, "Gotcha! See, you can get quiet if you want to. Now while I've got your attention, I'm going to sing you a torch song." After performing in clubs for almost three decades, I had certainly learned how to grab the audience's attention.

Some people feel that when performers become successful they must give up their privacy: Their fame is their fortune, so anything is up for grabs. I disagree. While I am always willing to sign autographs, be photographed, or give an interview, I believe that there are certain aspects of a celebrity's life that no one is unconditionally entitled to have. Medical history is certainly at the top of that list. In 1991, our cast and crew were confronted with a situation that was sadly becoming quite popular in the tabloid press: outing actors who were HIV+. It was a spectator sport I particularly despised.

# TWELVE

# I'm Just Getting Started

*I*n the spring of 1991, a young actor named Joe Breen joined the cast of *World*. He had been hired to play Scott, Lisa's long-lost son, as a new source of conflict for the show. The way in which the character was created is a perfect illustration of how our head writer, Doug Marland, utilized an actor's input to create a new story line.

Doug telephoned me one evening to discuss what he said was something new and exciting for Lisa.

"Eileen, I want to bring in another character and I want him to be your son. Is it possible that Chucky didn't really die? Do you think he could have been kidnapped by John Eldridge?"

"I don't think so, Doug," I replied. "Nancy buried that boy and when Nancy buries someone, they stay dead. There's no way he could have been scooped up alive and carried away. But I was off the show for a year when I married John Eldridge. Maybe something happened while I was away."

"Now that's an interesting idea," he slowly said while he began working out new plot ideas in his head. "What happened in the marriage?"

"The audience never really knew. Irna never wrote about it. She always wanted to get on with the new story line and not talk about what had already happened. So whenever anyone asked me about John Eldridge I said, 'Oh, I don't want to talk about him.' The only detail that really emerged from that period was that when I returned, I was very wealthy and very glamorous."

"Well, then, you got paid off!" Doug said, the plot details beginning to fall into place. "You had a baby by John Eldridge, he blackmailed you and bought the baby, and that's when you returned to Oakdale! I'll write you a terrific story line and create your son!"

And that's how Scott was born.

I had such a fun time playing myself in flashback scenes from my days with John Eldridge, wearing old clothes and hairstyles. It was like visiting a familiar friend I hadn't seen for years. We introduced the plot line and then brought Scott in as a young man. I remember in our earliest scenes, Scott didn't know Lisa was his mother—he began flirting with her, and she had to quickly set him straight. The audience loved it.

And I loved working with Joe. We had a wonderful time "fighting" our way through many confrontational mother and son scenes.

Approximately six months after Joe began working on our show, the *Enquirer* printed an article announcing that he was HIV+. I can't remember who their source was or why they felt it was so newsworthy, but the paper gave the story the full tabloid banner treatment. The night before the paper hit the stands, Laurie Caso, our executive producer, telephoned me: "Eileen, I have some terrible news about Joe. I wanted you to know the truth before you hear about it from anyone else."

I'll never forget the day the issue hit the stands. Everyone at the studio just felt awful. No one wanted to believe the article, but we felt it would have been inappropriate to discuss it with Joe or, even, among ourselves.

That very day, Laurie called a meeting and requested that

everyone—actors, writers, crew, office personnel—attend. Laurie is a very wise and wonderful gentleman who has always treated the cast with dignity and respect. He felt that the only way to handle what had happened was to put it out in the open. He knew the fastest way to end the "whispers by the water cooler" was to have everyone—including Joe—talk about what was happening at the same time. We were fortunate to have someone with his sensitivity in charge at the time—and we're lucky he's still with us today.

I felt sorry for Joe and angry that anyone felt he had the right to violate that aspect of an actor's privacy for the sole purpose of selling newspapers. I'm the last one to complain about the press—tabloid or not. They all serve a purpose, and I've certainly used the columns and papers to benefit my career at times. But everyone has to draw the line somewhere—define his or her own standards that determine what the public has a right to know about a celebrity. In my filing system of life, medical information is in the same folder as confessions to a priest, discussions with a psychiatrist, and advice from an attorney: They must all be considered privileged and confidential information. Once that privacy had been violated, however, the story had to be confronted, questions needed to be answered.

When everyone had arrived for the meeting, Joe stood in front of the group and began speaking in a calm, quiet voice.

"I'm sorry to have to tell you this, but, yes, it's true. I am HIV+, but I'm fine. I'm alive and well and working in Oakdale with a wonderful and crazy group of people and I appreciate your concern, but as of today I'm okay."

When Joe finished speaking, Laurie assured him that he had the love and support of the entire show in his corner. "Just remember," he concluded. "You're not alone in this. We will always be there for you."

I felt proud to be a part of *World* that day, and I felt so lucky to have an executive in charge with such a strong sense of humanity. When I left the studio, I wondered how another show or company or business would have handled the situation if it suddenly became front page news that one of its employees was infected with the AIDS virus. Would they have been so supportive and compassionate? Would they have tried to make the situation "disappear" by terminating the employee? Ignore the rumor or allow it to become fodder for lunch room gossip? I was convinced that very few organizations would have tackled the situation head-on.

We put the unpleasant way the information came out on the back burner and tried to be as loving and supportive as we could. Actresses assured the writers and producers that they had no problem playing love scenes with Joe. One of the most ironic and difficult aspects for him was that *World* was in the midst of an AIDS-related story line. Margo was raped by a man who was HIV+. For weeks, she agonized, wondering if she, too, would contract the virus. Joe had to play scenes with her, reassuring Margo that she wasn't going to die, telling her she'd be fine, that she shouldn't be afraid to hug her son or see her friends. Everything he said had a double meaning. Eventually, Margo's test results came back negative and the story line ended.

Unfortunately, a few months later, Joe's condition seemed to deteriorate. He began to lose weight and was frequently sick. It was just so sad! I kept wondering to what extent the pressure he was under, being exposed in such a publicly humiliating manner, and being scrutinized at every turn, contributed toward his degeneration. I also wondered if the editors of tabloid newspapers and the readers who devoured this specific story were in any way troubled by the possibility that their thirst to know or to tell cost someone a day or even an hour of life. Or by the fact that the quality of whatever time Joe had remaining was diminished by having his illness exposed against his will.

He couldn't sneeze or cough or get a cold sore without it having some added meaning. I kept vascillating, trying to decide what was the right thing to do: ask him how he was doing if he didn't look well or just ignore the situation for fear of overreacting. Joe was thrust into a no-win situation. At one point I thought, *Can you imagine what it's like for someone who* doesn't *have the love or support of family, friends, and fellow employees at a time like this?* We were all trying to help him as best we could, but I could see it wasn't enough.

As Joe's condition further deteriorated, he became increasingly hostile. He was obviously angry about not just what was happening inside his body but how society itself was judging him for his illness—and ultimately, I believe, how he judged himself. He began having irrational outbursts, hurling insults at co-workers for no apparent reason. Of course, he always apologized afterward. Eventually, he left the show. Another actor on *World* told me he recently saw Joe at an actor's convention and that he looked terrific. I certainly hope it's true.

It's always difficult when an actor, producer, or writer departs under such unpleasant circumstances. And when one of the cast or crew dies, it's like losing a member of your family—especially if it's someone who's been on the soap for years. When Don McLaughlin passed away, everyone felt like we had lost one of the corner stones of our foundation. Of course, the producers couldn't replace him—the viewers would have never accepted a new Chris after so many years.

Laurie Caso decided to create a story line about what happens if after a long and happy marriage you become a widow and then suddenly find yourself attracted to someone new. Helen began a romance with a kindhearted gentleman, confronted her feelings of guilt and loyalty to Chris, and eventually remarried. Our older viewers—anyone over thirty these days—certainly enjoyed following the slow and careful courtship that led up to the wedding. Her new husband, played brilliantly by Dan Frazer, had a story line where his character developed Alzheimer's disease. The writers wanted to educate our audience about its tell-tales signs and various forms of treatment and help currently available.

In 1992, *World* endured another painful loss: the terrible tragedy that occurred when one of our young actors, Michael Morrison, died of a drug overdose. Michael was such a talented young man. When he first joined the cast, I adored working with him. He had pretty brown eyes, a cute little turned-up nose, and dimples. I thought he was just precious. He had a marvelous sense of humor and loved telling me jokes on the set.

"Oh, Leenie," he'd squeal with delight, "did you hear the one about the touring actor who . . ." His body was constantly moving, fidgeting, twitching. I always attributed it to nervous energy and certainly never suspected chemical abuse. The kids on the set knew what was going on, but they never breathed a word to me. I'm sure they thought they had to protect me: "Don't tell Eileen, she's led a sheltered life."

I first became concerned and then later angry when Michael's condition deteriorated to the point where I dreaded our scenes together: He would arrive late and smelling of alcohol, and he could be very edgy and hostile. Instead of entertaining me with his jokes, Michael began firing insults and attacks.

"You want to run this scene or not," he would snarl. "It's up to you. It's your career. I know what *I'm* doing."

The most amazing thing was the moment the cameras began rolling, he zeroed in on exactly what he needed to be doing. It was as if he could flip a switch and pull it together in a matter of seconds if he had to. The moment the scene ended, however, he continued the "bad boy" routine. Everyone wanted to help him—to save him—but I've learned you can't save someone who doesn't want to be saved. Michael eventually went to one of those clinics and came back looking young and vital and relaxed. But in a matter of weeks he was back to where he started.

The producers were very patient with Michael and tried to help him through a difficult time. I have to admit I've seen them fire actors or crew members for what I thought were the most ridiculous reasons, but whenever someone had a real problem—a destructive problem—they stuck by that individual for as long as possible.

The night before Michael's death, I had a frightening dream. I was standing on the ledge of a castle cradling Michael in my arms. He was just a small child. There were hundreds of white birds everywhere staring at us. I began to carry him down the path, but I stopped because I saw a large black bird with magnificent red and yellow wings. Everything froze for a very long time. I tried to get Michael past this amazing bird, but I couldn't. It was very unsettling.

I woke up the next morning exhausted and thought I had the dream because I was not looking forward to working with Michael that day. By the time I walked into the rehearsal hall, I was in a particularly foul mood. Michael hadn't arrived, so we assumed he was running late again. Forty-five minutes passed and he still hadn't arrived, and I decided I'd had enough of his unprofessional behavior.

"Well, damnit. Let's just forget the scene," I snapped. "We're running long today, it's not important. I don't want to waste any more time." As I mentioned, I wasn't in a particularly forgiving mood that morning.

Several hours later, I had a break and strolled up to the studio office. As I walked through the corridor, I could feel the chill of tragedy in the air. I walked into the office and saw several people huddled closely around a desk, whispering. I could tell from their faces that something terrible had occurred.

"What's wrong?" I asked. "What's the matter?"

No one spoke for a few seconds. Everyone exchanged glances, trying to silently decide who the messenger would be. Finally one of the writers stepped forward.

"It's Michael."

"Yes, I know. Old Michael—late again! We had to cut the scene. So what happened? Was he in some kind of accident?"

"No, Eileen. He's dead. He overdosed in some girl's apartment downtown."

I couldn't believe it. It was like another fantastic plot twist on a soap. Whenever people criticize our show and say the story lines are farfetched and unbelievable I tell them, "You've either led a privileged life or you haven't talked to enough people to find out what really happens 'out there.' " What actually happens in real life is always more bizarre than anything anyone could ever make up.

I began to feel horribly guilty for my behavior that morning. It was all so sad and such a waste. All I could do was picture that adorable, funny, talented boy who first arrived on our set. What happened? What went wrong?

Young actors like Michael can have an especially difficult time adjusting to their newfound fame and fortune. A contract role on a daytime soap can be worth hundreds of thousands of dollars, depending on how well the character takes off and if you move into the lucrative world of personal appearances. To a thirty-one-year-old who's used to surviving on three hundred dollars a week, that's a lot of expendable cash. If you lack a certain common sense, discipline, and the ability to say "no"— to quote Miss Nancy, the infamous lady-in-red—it's very easy to wade into that sea of temptations and start drifting downriver.

When I started working on soaps, actors were *never* late. They arrived ready to work, didn't fool around on the set or slow down production, and rarely acted like prima donnas. I don't mean to imply that we never fought for what we believed was right for a scene or questioned the director at times. God knows I've done my share of asking questions.

Sometimes that behavior is misunderstood—especially if it's a woman doing the asking. A few years ago when Marisa Tomei, the Academy Award-winning actress for *My Cousin Vinny,* was on our show, she continually fought for what she thought was right. Some people misunderstood her intentions. When the director would stage the scene in a way she felt was wrong for her character, she would announce, "I feel that I should do this line standing up. I can't say this sitting down. I have to stand up!"

I knew exactly how she felt and it reminded me of a very young Eileen Fulton many years ago. I loved her for her feisty, fighting spirit and stood up for her behavior at times when other cast members criticized her for being difficult.

Being one of the old-timers, I frequently take young actors aside. I'll confide to them, "Look, I know how you feel because I've been there. But you have to understand it from the director's perspective. If you're going to disagree, you have to have a very specific reason for why you can't do the action as directed and then offer an alternative way that will satisfy everyone. And you have to do it quickly."

I learned early on during the days of live television that there is no time to fight on the set. Some actors will go off on a tangent and not realize that their "fit" is extending what is already a very long day for everyone. There are basically two ways to get what you want: you either have to be so powerful with huge ratings and an enormous salary to match that no one would dare challenge you; or you can be charming and act reasonably. Of course, a combination of both is even better.

During my first year on *World,* I kept getting annoyed with a prop man who would jingle change in his pocket while we were on the air. The more intense the scene became, the faster and louder he jingled. By this point, I had learned *not* to yell at anyone to get what I wanted—especially the crew. I approached the "currency counter" after we had finished for the day and tried to charm him into changing habits.

"Excuse me, Ralph. I hate to bother you, but I concentrate so fiercely during my scenes that the smallest things can rattle me. You know those coins in your pocket? Well, if they were bills, I'd have an easier time of it. A rich man like you should be counting hundreds instead of those measly little nickles and dimes."

He laughed and apologized—and never did it again. Of course, if people are out and out rude, I'm not above telling them to shut up. But if someone is unintentionally creating a disturbance, I always try a more diplomatic approach.

I was not so diplomatic, however, when I appeared on *Geraldo!* a few years ago. I've done his show several times. Once the topic was "Famous Women in Show Business Who've Survived Multiple Marriages" or some soul-searching topic like that. Lorna Luft was one of the guests, and we traded horror stories. I wore all of my "husband rings"—my wedding rings—because I thought the audience would get a kick out of it.

The last time I appeared on *Geraldo!* the show was all about "The Casting Couch: What Was It Like Before; Does It Still Exist?" It just so happened that the day I was going to tape the show, *Celebrity Sleuth* (a must-read magazine for gossip mongers) came out with an issue that pictured a naked girl who resembled me. The caption read: "Can this be *our* Eileen Fulton?" It made me so mad! It didn't even look like me: The mole was in the wrong spot and the teeth were crooked.

The moment I got onto Geraldo's set, I started telling the audience what had happened. I looked straight into the camera and said, "Let me tell everyone right here, right now, that is *not* a picture of Eileen Fulton. I can assure you that if Eileen Fulton had posed for a picture like that, she would be wearing a pair of drop-dead fabulous earrings!" The audience loved it.

Once my professional reputation had been cleared up, we began a discussion of the casting couch system. One of the panel members was some "actress" named Sally who was convinced that the only way to get ahead was by getting into a reclining position. I took great exception to her attitude.

"That's not how respectable actresses work. You don't have to do that. You don't have to sell yourself just to get a job. Period! I got where I am on my talent—not on my back!"

"Well, I don't think we're hearing the whole story," she retorted. "How exactly *did* you get on the soap? Are you sure there weren't a few nighttime auditions?"

I leapt out of my chair yelling, "How dare you say that to me!" She started climbing out of her chair, so I assumed a karate position and was ready to "kung-fu" the silly cow if she got within a foot of me. Geraldo quickly put a stop to our wrestling match.

The incident was in all the newspapers and CBS ended up using the clip for their fall promos. After a voice announced "Geraldo is coming to CBS," they flashed to the clip of me in a karate position yelling, "How dare you say that to me!"

Although I've never won an Emmy, I certainly have received my fair share of awards through the years. The first time they had awards for daytime television performers was in 1973, many years before the creation of the Daytime Emmy Awards. The ceremony was not going to be televised, because no one at the time thought the viewing audience would be interested. I was very nervous, because I knew I was going to receive a special award and Irna was going to present it to me. At that point, I had just instigated my "Granny Clause" and Irna was angry. We weren't speaking. I was afraid she might say something terrible about me in front of everyone.

The ceremony took place in a Manhattan restaurant. I invited my parents for moral support and hoped for the best. All through the dinner and subsequent ceremony, Irna was giving me looks from across the room. My award was the last to be presented that night, and by the time Irna stood up and walked to the podium, I was a nervous wreck. My mind kept racing for something clever to say, but I drew a blank. The room grew silent before Irna spoke. She was one of the most respected writer-producers in daytime. Just before she started to talk, she looked at me and smiled.

"I'm giving this award tonight," she began, "to this particular actress because she is Eileen Fulton. There is only one Eileen Fulton and there will never be another like her again!"

I broke into tears. She was so kind and gracious. Of all the awards I've been given through the years, that first one, handed to me by Irna herself, still means the most.

In 1976 I received an award for "Favorite Female Serial Actress," presented to me on *The Dinah Shore Show.* And in 1991, *Soap Opera Digest* honored me with the "Editor's Award." I fought for many years to have the Daytime Emmy Awards televised at night, but always encountered resistance. Since the instigation of the Emmys, I've been nominated once—didn't win—but I'm not finished yet, so who knows?

I continued my club singing and working with Vinnie Martucci, my wonderful piano player, Charlie Knicley, my bass player, and the adorable Charlie Morano as my drummer. The first time the three of us worked together was in Greensboro, North Carolina, in 1991 when I returned to my college to give a concert. You can't imagine how exciting it was to return to the school where I had studied music to sing for hundreds of people. The audience was enthusiastic and everyone treated me like visiting royalty. Before the performance, they held a magnificent dinner in the reception room of my old dormitory, which looked as lovely as ever.

I was having such fun working with "Vinnie and the Charlies"—which is how I referred to them—I decided to cut a demo record, which eventually convinced me to record an entire album. On December 18, 1992, in the midst of one of the worst snow storms of the year, I drove to Long Island to record *First Kiss* on my newly formed label, Starlight. I thought it would be easy to distribute the finished product on my own by placing a small advertisement in *Soap Opera Magazine*. The response was overwhelming. For several months, my New York apartment was transformed into a warehouse for distributing the CDs and cassettes. I had more boxes and labels lining my floor than a UPS center. I soon realized that I couldn't handle the situation on my own.

My record producer advised me to utilize the services of a fulfillment house to distribute *First Kiss* and located a small family-run organization in Florida. CBS decided to help promote the recording by sending me on a short media tour through the South. I was scheduled to appear on various television and radio programs where I would be able to announce the 800 number of the fulfillment house.

One of my first stops was a television station in Charlotte, North Carolina. I was going to appear on the morning show, bake my mama's corn bread, and promote the record, telling everyone, "Whenever I cook I like to listen to some good music." Just before air time, the producers ran up to me looking about as nervous as a group of turkeys on Thanksgiving Eve.

"Eileen, uh, do you . . . are you . . ." one of them began stuttering.

"What? What is it?"

"Are you sure this 800 number of yours is correct?"

I didn't know what they were getting at. I read the number on the paper. "Yes, that's it. That's the one we're using."

"Well, do The Jerky Boys mean anything to you?"

My memory flashed for a second to a pair of red-headed twin boys who used to tease me in Asheville, but I knew she wasn't talking about them. And then I remembered that the fulfillment house had once mentioned that name. They also filled orders for that particular comedy rap group. "All I know is my distributor handles them. Why?"

"Well," the producer continued while she stared at my feet, "we called the 800 number. They put us on hold and played some of The Jerky Boys. We got an earful of four-letters words and heard what we could do with many of our private body parts. I'm sorry, Eileen, but this is a Mother's Day show. We can't let you use this number. Our viewers would be offended if they heard that recording."

I was more embarrassed than the time one of my eyelashes fell off during a taping and landed in a glass of wine. "Of course," I assured them. "I understand. Don't worry. I won't mention the number."

I immediately telephoned my lawyers. After several weeks of legal maneuvering, I was able to get my supply of CDs and cassettes returned and am currently planning on selling the record on one of the shopping channels or through the use of an "Infomercial." I've certainly had my fill of fulfillment houses!

For the past few years, I've been trying to concentrate more on my singing, performing my club act from New York's Supper Club to the Cinegrill in Los Angeles. Whenever I travel anywhere to do my club act, I always take my dear assistant, Kenneth, along. He not only helps me maintain my sanity during the most stressful times, but he's also a genius with hair and makeup and is a gourmet cook to boot! I met him through my publicist, David Granoff. The day he walked into my apartment, I knew he was the right man for the job, because my terribly shy Shitzu, Sisi (short for Simone Signoret), took one look at Kenneth and his pony tail and jumped right in his lap and began licking his face. I guess she thought he was a long-lost relative.

My engagement at the Cinegrill in 1992 was a very big occasion. Many of my Los Angeles soap friends, like Jeanne Cooper from *The Young and the Restless,* and Darlene Connally from *The Bold and the Beautiful,* came to see the show. The day I opened, flowers kept arriving at the Roosevelt Hotel.

I had just finished putting on a face mask cream that, when it dries, makes it impossible for me to speak—not to mention the fact that it makes me look like my skin has been burnt to a crisp. The concierge telephoned to announce that more flowers had arrived, and I told him to send them up. When the bellman knocked, I stood behind the door so he wouldn't see my face and pointed to a side table where I wanted him to place the flowers. Before he had a chance to set them down, I realized I should give him a tip. I forgot about my face and ran to retrieve my purse. When I handed him his tip, he took one look at my mask-covered face, which by this point was beginning to crack, and went into shock.

"Now, don't worry," I said in my most reassuring tone. "It's Nu-skin." (Nu-skin was the brand name of the product.)

He nodded in agreement and said in a Chinese accent, "Ah, we need new skin. Yes, good idea."

He must have thought I had rushed out to one of Los Angeles's infamous plastic surgeons for an emergency face peel hours before my opening!

I find singing one of the most satisfying creative experiences. Each song is a different character with different loves, losses, and laments. God knows I've suffered through enough of Lisa's—as well as my own! After over three decades of living in Oakdale, Lisa Miller Hughes Eldridge Shea Coleman (almost Hadley) McColl Mitchell has reached a plateau. Whether from age or the fact that she's "done it all," Lisa is not as active as she once was, creating havoc, destroying lives. As an actress, I try to find as much life as I can in my scenes to help keep her going, but I would be lying if I didn't admit that I miss the days of playing that scheming, conniving, seductive, manipulative, glamorous bitch!

Believe me, I don't mean to complain. I'm grateful for the wonderful opportunities *World* has offered me and believe after so many years the producers and I have come to appreciate and respect each other.

But, of course, I want more! Actors are like children at a restaurant, not liking or appreciating the wonderful food that they have been given but eyeing the dessert that someone else has at the next table. We always want to be doing more or are looking toward that next job, character, or plot line.

And if you look hard and long enough, you sometimes get it. Being on a soap, one never knows what's in store, where that next plot twist might take you—which dangerous Caribbean island you might find yourself stranded on, or when that long-lost son you forgot about during your last bout of amnesia will suddenly reappear.

Soaps, like life itself, are full of unexpected twists and turns and surprises. They've been around in one form or another for hundreds of years. And as long as the writers don't veer too far off the original course—or try to be too far out—I'm certain they'll be around for hundreds more. Back in the sixties and seventies, when our show was really hot, we dealt primarily with two families and the conflicting relationships and struggles between them. It's basically the original creative formula for all storytelling: protagonist versus antagonist in a conflict with a little bit of sex and a lot of romance thrown in to spice things up! It's a formula that still works today. Unfortunately, we have so many characters and so many plot lines, it's hard sometimes to keep it all straight.

If you think about what made the nighttime soaps (*Dallas, Dynasty*) so popular, it was the same concept, but they added business back-biting and glamour. When the nighttime soaps were taking off our show started getting bizarre and gimmicky with unusual characters such as dwarfs or plot twists such as time travel. Although the viewers may have initially found these devices fascinating, they quickly lost interest.

Once, when we flashed our characters back to Edwardian times, I received a letter from a woman asking me what had happened. She wrote: "I went out to the kitchen to get a sandwich during the commercial and when I came back I was convinced something weird had happened to my television. Everyone was in low-cut gowns from another century with their bosoms hanging out and bustles bulging in the back. People's faces were the same but they spoke with accents. I don't get what's going on." Well, to be honest, neither did I.

I do miss the old days when we had long two-character scenes in which we could really get into it and take the audience along with us. Everything moves faster today: two-minute scenes, large groups, and quick cuts. I think because of this fast-paced, fast-food, MTV, channel-flicking culture of ours, the writers and producers think our audience will get bored. I disagree.

But why do you think movies like *Sleepless in Seattle* or *Howards End* were so popular? How do you explain the phenomenal success of a book like *The Bridges of Madison County?* I think there is a large segment of the population that hungers for subtle, relationship-driven entertainment—stories that focus on what happens between two people, filled with romance, longing, and emotional hunger. As long as soaps don't forget that their success is rooted in relationships, they'll go on forever!

People often ask me, "What was it like playing a bitch for so long? Didn't you get tired of it?" The answer has always been a resounding, "No! Not for a second!" As Lisa I lied and hurt people and put them in such a horrible state that I destroyed their lives and caused them to commit suicide. That is the kind of despicable person I portrayed. My whole reason for acting is to create a different life, to live the character, be the character. It's like giving birth.

As I stated, those really were the good ol' days when a gal could sink her claws into a guy or two, then spit him out and lick her chops for one more. I was the first bitch to ever last. And the secret was to find something good about that person, something vulnerable.

Look at Lisa, for example. What made her really work was the fact that no matter how wonderfully wicked she was to her husbands, enemies, and lovers, she truly loved her children and would have sacrificed anything for them. That saved her—redeemed her for the viewers. For an actor, it's the most exciting thing in the world to play the villain (or villainess) because you drive the plot—it's so alive! Let's face it, it sure beats sitting around a kitchen table complaining about how that wonderful guy you just met hasn't called.

For the first time in my life, I've reached the stage where I'm handling everything on my own. No husbands. No managers. No one to shape or guide my personal or professional life. I view my past journeys as a road map to the present, which, in turn, will lead to many wonderful, exciting, and (as of yet) undiscovered countries. I certainly don't view any of my choices—even when it comes to men—with second thoughts or regrets. And I never think of my life in terms of sacrifices. The sacrifice would have been if I'd done what everyone else did in order to be a "normal" girl from the South. If I'd have done that, I wouldn't be where I am today. For me, *that* would have been a sacrifice.

But I'll admit I've made some poor decisions about men, because there have been times over the years when I was overly romantic or just plain lonely. I would get married or have some kind of wild love affair that was just totally stupid when I look back on it now. I'm just glad I didn't marry everybody I've been madly in love with, or I'd be paying too much alimony!

This past year, I've been trying to get my life together by focusing on my career: where it was, where it is now, and where I want to take it. I gave up my house in Connecticut, surrounded by trees and birds, because I feel *now* is the time for me to be here—in Manhattan—pursuing my goals. There's a lyric from a song I perform at the end of my nightclub act, written by Peggy Lee and Cy Coleman, which best expresses my current philosophy:

> *Then was then*
> *And now is now*
> *Don't look back*
> *You can't look back somehow*
> *Sweet was sweet*
> *But not so bitter now*
> *Then was then*
> *And now is now*
>
> *Now we can win*
> *No matter what might have been*
> *Now we can begin again*
> *For then was then*
> *And now is now*

As my world keeps turning, I take satisfaction from the fact that *I'm* now the one who makes it revolve. I'm setting myself up for the next exciting chapter of my life. On my own. Acting. Singing. I want to do a Broadway show again. Record another album. Sing all over the world. Just thinking about all of the exhilarating adventures I have yet to live gives me goose bumps! It's hard to believe that I'm celebrating my thirty-fifth year on *As the World Turns*. Thirty-five years! Can you imagine that! But you know what?

I'm really just getting started.

# INDEX